Chip Carver's Workbook

by Dennis Moor

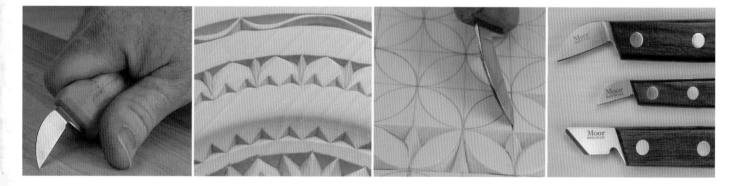

Teach Yourself with 7 Easy and Decorative Projects

Fox
Chapel Publishing

1970 Broad Street • East Petersburg, PA 17520
www.FoxChapelPublishing.com

Dedication

There is nothing like grandchildren, and, of course, my three are the best: Emilee, Turtle, and Zane. This book is dedicated to the three of them.

Acknowledgments

My son, Todd, is largely responsible for my dedication to this art and to Chipping Away. His encouragement and involvement with our business included countless hours of traveling, teaching, exhibiting, and, of course, carving. We worked wonderfully together.

Chip Carver's Workbook is an original work, first published in 2005 by Fox Chapel Publishing Company, Inc. The patterns contained herein are copyrighted by the author. Readers may make three copies of these patterns for personal use. The patterns themselves, however, are not to be duplicated for resale or distribution under any circumstances. Any such copying is a violation of copyright law.

ISBN: 978-1–56523–257–0

Publisher's Cataloging-in-Publication Data

Moor, Dennis.
    Chip carver's workbook : teach yourself with 7 easy and decorative projects / by Dennis Moor. East Petersburg, PA : Fox Chapel Publishing, c2005.

        p. ; cm.
        ISBN-13: 978-1–56523–257–0
        ISBN-10: 1–56523–257–7

        1. Wood-carving. 2. Carving (Decorative arts) I. Title.
TT199.7 .M66 2005
736/.4--dc22   0504

To learn more about the other great books from Fox Chapel Publishing, or to find a retailer near you, call toll-free 800-457-9112 or visit us at **www.FoxChapelPublishing.com.**

Note to Authors: We are always looking for talented authors to write new books in our area of woodworking, design, and related crafts. Please send a brief letter describing your idea to Acquisition Editor, 1970 Broad Street, East Petersburg, PA 17520.

First Printing: May 2005
Second Printing: September 2006
Third Printing: September 2008

CONTENTS

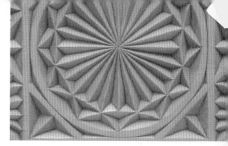

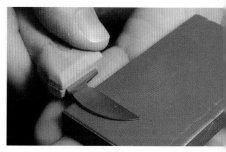

Dennis "Pop" Moor has taken the carving world by storm, winning numerous international awards. He and his son, Todd's, weekly television series has introduced viewers to all areas of woodcarving and wood art and has helped to establish the duo as highly sought-after personalities at woodcarving shows and competitions. Because of the entertaining approach they take to their art, this father-son team has earned an excellent reputation in carving, teaching, and judging. It is no wonder these two are often called "The Canadian Masters."

Dennis is the president of Chipping Away Incorporated, which he started with Todd. More than just a retail company, Chipping Away publishes books, manufactures woodcarving tools and sharpening machines, writes articles for magazines, and sells some of their 4,000 products to smaller retailers by acting as a distributor for a number of companies. They have customers in 20 countries around the world. Chipping Away also operates two large classrooms at their Kitchener, Ontario, Resource Center with both evening and weekend classes in all aspects of woodcarving, woodburning and wood art. In addition to their local instructors, they host some of the top woodcarving instructors from across North America. Chipping Away also sponsors an annual International Carver's Conference each September.

To keep his multifaceted company going, Dennis consistently works 60 plus hours each week. He leaves each night with a smile on his face and can hardly wait to return the next morning. *Wood Carving Illustrated*'s T-shirts that read, "Eat, Sleep, Carve" describe Pop perfectly. Dennis and his wife, Joani, have been married for 42 years and have two daughters, both older than Todd, three grandchildren, and three step-grandchildren.

CHIP CARVING IN TYPICAL CHIPPING AWAY STYLE

EASIER THAN YOU MIGHT THINK

by Todd Moor

As life gets more complex and stressful, I find myself more appreciative of the simple escapes it offers. One such blessing I have is a hobby that has turned into a full-time profession. Chip carving has a long history of use in decorating various wooden household items, including furniture, as well as in creating purely artistic pieces. Although the finished chip-carved pieces often display an intricacy and beauty one may think is attainable only by a long-lived master carver, chip carving can be surprisingly easy to learn. My father deserves much of the credit for this. He taught me a simple and effective method for chip carving a limitless variety of designs. Working together, we have taught this chip carving method to well over 2,000 students worldwide. Our chip carving students have included both men and women, from adolescents to octogenarians and all ages in between. I have seen some hold skepticism as to whether or not they could chip carve, and keep in mind that I have never met a person who cannot.

DEFINITION OF CHIP CARVING

Chip carving is a style of woodcarving in which knives are used to remove selected "chips" of wood from the project in a single piece. In theory, chip carvings have just two levels, or planes: the wood surface and the point beneath the surface where the cuts meet. Patterns can be free-form style or geometrically based with figures, such as triangles, circles, simple lines, and curves. If we accept this definition of chip carving, we find that almost every society throughout history has experimented with it, which makes the precise origins of chip carving debatable. It has been my experience that the strongest factor in such arguments is usually the nationality of the debater. I believe that this simple definition of chip carving allows us to consider that it originated in various societies without the necessity of influence from other groups. I find comfort in the notion that chip carving has a rich and long history for all of us, deep in our common cultural identities.

There are variations in the tools and designs favored by chip carvers of various cultural backgrounds. My father and I have a simple approach to understanding chip carving that offers the advantages of minimizing both the number of tools and rules the student needs to learn. In fact, I've found the reasons underlying such "rules" are worthy of greater emphasis than the rules themselves. There are times when the rules must be broken, and a good understanding of chip carving will help you know when to break them.

POP'S TEN COMMANDMENTS FOR CHIP CARVERS

Say, I don't believe I have told you why so many call me "Pop." During the early days of Chipping Away, my son, Todd, and I exhibited at wood shows and taught classes together. Todd has always called me "Pop," and whenever he would holler "Hey, Pop!" across a room, it didn't take long for others to join in. While I was teaching a class at the Thunder Mountain Wood Carvers Club in Sierra Vista, Arizona, Don Yadusky, a student in the class, kept lots of notes. At the close of the class, he announced that by using his observations, he created "Pop's Ten Commandments for Chip Carvers." I would like to share them with you.

1 Remove the largest chips first.

2 Carve those areas that are the most delicate (sharp ridges) last.

3 When carving rosettes, start with cuts that are diagonal to the grain and move in one direction only. Using this progression, you will remove the more difficult cross-grained chips before finishing with the easier, with-the-grain ones.

4 When carving into the center of a rosette, roll your knife up to almost 90 degrees. This technique will keep the center from chipping out, especially in those patterns where you will be carving into the center a number of times.

5 If you have trouble removing large chips with one cut, then carve in stages. You will find that by taking smaller chips out of the center of the large one and gradually increasing the size, the final chip will be much easier to remove. Your carving will also be much neater and cleaner.

6 When starting a new chip, always make the first cut with the blade facing away from your previous chip.

7 Make use of stop cuts.

8 Keep your thumb against the handle blade and on the wood at all times. This thumb position will ensure consistent angles and will minimize the chance of cutting yourself.

9 Always look for ways to add that final touch or embellishment—create the "ooohhs."

10 Have fun!

1

CHOOSING THE WOOD

WHICH WOOD IS BEST FOR CHIP CARVING?

It is certainly not difficult to understand that the harder the wood, the harder it is to carve. This does not mean, however, that softwoods are the easiest or best woods to use. It's also important to note that the terms "hardwood" and "softwood" don't necessarily reflect how hard the wood is. Some hardwoods are less dense or lighter than some softwoods.

Generally, any tree that loses its leaves in the fall, or a deciduous tree, is considered a hardwood. In contrast, softwoods, such as pine and spruce, retain their greenery year-round and are considered to be part of the coniferous family. Hardwood trees grow with a more consistent and tighter grain pattern than do softwood trees.

Thus, hardwoods give a more predictable response to your knives and gouges.

While hardwoods often have more density (weight per unit volume) than softwoods, density varies widely between species. Poplar and aspen, for example, are much lighter in weight than oak, but oak is lighter in weight than rosewood and most exotic woods. Let's take a look at the qualities of some popular carving woods.

Basswood (hardwood)

Chances are, if you are not a woodcarver, you are not familiar with basswood. The basswood tree is also known as linden in Canada and the U.S. Basswood is considered to be the best carving

Figure 1-1. Basswood.

wood regardless of what style of carving you may be doing. The grain is consistently tight, and the timber is light in weight, which makes it a joy to carve (See **Figure 1-1**.). The light beige or yellow color, combined with the almost non-existent grain, allows intricate or detailed carving to be performed without the carving and the wood competing for attention.

The American basswood tree grows in fair abundance from the southern U.S. to a hundred miles or so north of the Canadian/U.S. border, from about the central states through to the East Coast. Generally speaking, the best "carving basswood" grows in the latitude area of southern Michigan (including southern Ontario) south to Kentucky and in the longitude area from Iowa east to the coast. Basswood growing north of this region tends to grow too slowly and is harder to carve. Similarly, in the areas south of Kentucky, it grows too quickly and is not as firm. Poplar and aspen are often used in western North America as substitutes for basswood.

Butternut (hardwood)

The butternut tree, also known as white walnut, grows in a geographical area similar to that of basswood. It is approximately 20% heavier in weight than basswood and carves easily with few surprises. Butternut has both a darker color and a more dominant grain pattern than basswood (See **Figure 1-2**.). Carvers use these characteristics to their benefit when the project will be left with a clear or light stain finish.

Figure 1-2. Butternut.

Mahogany (hardwood)

Mahogany (See **Figure 1-3**.) can certainly be chip carved should the occasion arise. While it isn't the most desirable wood to carve, a woodworker will find mahogany pleasant to work with and suitable for a number of projects. It may be that mahogany is chosen to match other pieces of furniture within a room. It is heavier than butternut and therefore is harder to chip carve, but it is workable. Keep the patterns simple.

Figure 1-3. Mahogany.

Avoid intricate or delicate patterns as well as sharp ridges or edges. Intricate patterns will not show up very well in mahogany, and sharp ridges or edges tend to break easily in this wood. Lettering shows up well on mahogany that has been stained.

Pine (softwood)

You will often find carvers using pine for small caricature or figure carvings. Pine's abundance and low cost, rather than its carving characteristics, are the reasons that many carvers choose this wood.

While pine can certainly be chip carved, it would not be my first choice for a couple of reasons. First, pine's consistency, or perhaps I should say "lack of consistency," of grain restricts the amount of fine or detail work that can be carved (See **Figure 1-4**.). Because the grain is not very tight, motifs that have sharp edges or ridges must be avoided to prevent breakouts (a ridge that breaks because it lacks rigidity) or fuzziness (See **Figure 1-5**.).

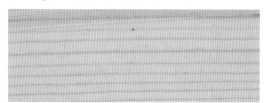

Figure 1-4. Pine.

Figure 1-5. Sharp edges, in designs such as this one, can break easily in some woods.

Figure 1-6. A basswood playing card box stained with Golden Oak. The box was made and carved by Jim Lindgren of Red Deer, Alberta.

Figure 1-7. This section is from a box lid carved in basswood. The lid was stained first with Mahogany and then with a coat of Cherry.

Figure 1-8. A section of a box lid carved in butternut and stained with Pecan.

Figure 1-9. These flowers are part of a small, decorative plaque carved in basswood and stained with Mahogany. The plaque was chip carved freehand and stained by Todd Moor.

Second, the darker grain in pine is much harder than the light-colored grain. You may not notice this characteristic when cutting pine using power tools or a hand saw, but if you draw a chip carving knife across the grain of a pine board, you will soon discover that it is very difficult to control your cuts.

This is not to say that you should avoid chip carving pine altogether. On the contrary, if you already own or are presented with pine items, such as a blanket chest, a toy box, or a set of shelves, you can certainly beautify these functional pieces with chip carving. Simply avoid sharp edges. A pine chest can soon become a cherished heirloom once you add a chip-carved name or a simple motif. If you have a choice, however, have the project made from basswood because it is much nicer to carve.

Other Woods

I guess you could chip carve just about any species of wood, but that does not mean you should. Obviously, the harder the wood is, the more difficult it will be to chip carve. Always ask yourself if the end result will really be worth the effort required.

If you have the task of chip carving a project to match another item, consider using basswood or butternut and then staining your project to match that item. It may surprise you how much butternut can be made to look like oak, walnut, pecan, and other woods once it is appropriately stained. Basswood can strikingly resemble maple, pine, or even cherry (See **Figure 1-6** to **Figure 1-9**.).

Chip Tip

When choosing the wood or item you wish to chip carve, make sure you consider the predominance of the grain. The more predominant the grain, the simpler your pattern should be. An intricate or busy pattern will compete with a heavily grained wood for attention, creating unpleasant results in both the appearance and the execution of the chips themselves.

Chip Tip

Wood with a moisture content of 10 to 12% is ideal for carving. If your wood is too dry, it will not carve as easily or as smoothly.

WOOD SOURCES

It is unlikely that you will find either basswood or butternut at your local home improvement center. Your local specialty lumber retailer will most likely have both species in stock. For those lucky enough to live in the geographic areas where basswood and butternut grow, a visit to a small lumber mill will provide all you need at reasonable prices. If you are still having problems finding a suitable supplier, get on the Internet and use a search engine to do a keyword search. It really is that simple.

MOISTURE AND WOOD

It is desirable to carve in wood that has an approximate moisture content of 10 to 12%. The correct moisture content not only makes your carving experience easier and more enjoyable, but it also produces a much nicer appearance. While there is no substitute for a properly sharpened and polished knife, you will find that dry wood does not cut as cleanly and that breakouts, especially on cross-grained chips, can be a challenge.

How can the layman determine the moisture content of the wood he is about to carve? You pretty much cannot tell, unless, of course, you invest in a quality moisture meter—something that is really not necessary. Once you make a few chips across the grain, you will be able to tell if the wood is too dry. Try using a test, or scrap, piece first. This way, if the wood is dry, you can take steps to return the moisture to it before beginning a project. It is also important to note that wood can have good moisture content when you purchase it but can become dry by the time you are ready to carve it.

An Ounce of Prevention

Storing your wood in a desirable manner will save you a good deal of frustration. Personally, I keep my stock of basswood in an unheated garage rather than in the house because a heated house will dry out the wood. Consider your geographic

A few things to keep in mind when storing your wood:
• Keep your wood in an unheated garage (or in a place suitable for your geographic region.
• If storing wood indoors, wrap it in airtight plastic or a similar airtight container.
• Keep it wrapped between carving sessions if you're concerned about the wood drying out.
• Don't store wood in your basement unless the room is humid and unheated.
• Don't store wood in your furnace room.
• Avoid storing wood in air-conditioned rooms because they remove moisture.

region when you're deciding where to store your wood. I live in southern Ontario, an area known for relatively high humidity. Those carvers living in drier climates, such as Arizona, would make different choices based on their location.

You may also want to take preventative measures if you're working on a project that will take more than a day or two to complete. I'll often return the project to my garage or make sure it is wrapped tightly in plastic between carving sessions, so the wood doesn't become too dry.

Returning Moisture to Your Wood

If you do find that your wood has lost too much moisture, there is a remedy. Returning moisture to your wood is as simple as building yourself a makeshift humidor and letting nature take its course.

To build a humidor, start by scavenging a cardboard box that is large enough to hold your wood board or project and small enough to fit inside a plastic bag. The large bags used for garbage are ideal.

Next, make a support to suspend your item and to permit airflow completely around it. A simple solution is to drive finishing nails through a thin piece of scrap plywood or similar material, so that the nails protrude enough to support your item (See **Figure 1-10** and **Figure 1-11**.).

Place your suspended item inside the cardboard box, which has had the top flaps removed or opened. Also place a small bowl containing a completely water-soaked sponge inside the box. Leave a small amount of water that the sponge cannot absorb in the bowl. Place the box and its contents inside the large plastic bag and use a twist tie to make an airtight seal.

Within two or three days, the wood will absorb all the moisture necessary and will be ready for carving. You can speed up the process by placing your humidor in direct sunlight, creating a miniature sauna; however, the moisture will not have the opportunity to penetrate as deeply as it would if the humidor were allowed to sit for two or three days.

Keep the large cardboard box handy—it will be useful when we are adding a finish to a project.

Warping Problems

Wood is subject to warping, or cupping, when it dries more quickly or absorbs moisture more quickly on one side or the other, especially if it's unsealed or unfinished. Chip carving projects are often affected by warping because many items are made of relatively thin wood (⅜") and have large surface areas, such as a serving tray.

In some cases, simply leaving your item with the cupped surface facing down can slowly rectify the problem. You could also try placing the item cupped-side-down on your lawn and in direct sunlight to speed up the process. The warmth of the sun's rays will help to draw moisture from the ground and into the piece of wood. Prevention of warping by not permitting such uneven drying is probably the best method; simply follow the suggestions for storing your wood.

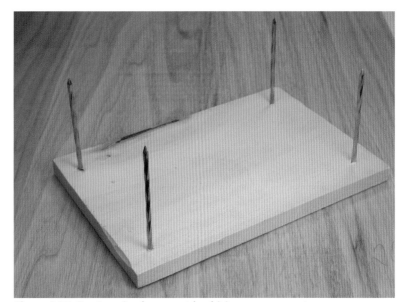

Figure 1-10. Create a simple support by driving finishing nails through a thin piece of plywood.

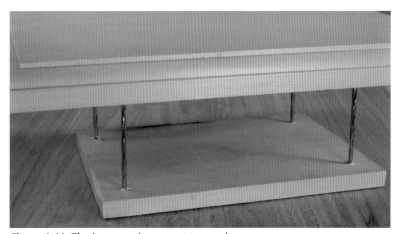

Figure 1-11. The homemade support suspends your wood and allows air to flow on all sides.

2

THE TOOLS

CHIP CARVING KNIVES

I often refer to "the simplicity of chip carving" in the context of both the tools used and the execution of the various cuts. It wasn't always simple. In earlier times, a variety of tools and knives were associated with the art, and the nationality of the carver generally determined which tools and methods were used.

Conventional carving knives are not suitable for chip carving because the blade does not have the appropriate angle (See **Figure 2-1**.). In the Netherlands, chip carvers used various razor-type blades; in Great Britain, they commonly used V-tools and single-beveled chisels and skews; and, in Scandinavia, they used various knives and chisels, in addition to picks, to clean out the

Figure 2-1. Conventional carving knives are not suitable for chip carving because the blade comes straight out from the handle without a downward angle.

bottoms of the cuts. One German tool manufacturer offers chip carving tool sets with as many as ten different shapes (See **Figure 2-2**.). Chip carving in these countries generally required the use of workbenches and holding devices, which obviously cut down on the portability of the art.

Figure 2-2. Seven of ten tools, specifically designed for chip carving, offered by a German company.

The Swiss Influence

Though they initially offered multiple tool sets, the Swiss eventually refined their approach to include only two basic tools. The main tool is a cutting knife, and the second tool is commonly called a stab knife. Wayne Barton, an American who is a well-known authority on chip carving, trained in Switzerland using these two basic tools (See **Figure 2-3** and **Figure 2-4**.).

Using just two tools surely made the art of chip carving much easier to learn as well as less expensive. Combine the simplicity of method with the fact that we require neither a workbench, nor clamps, nor a multitude of tools and aids generally associated with carving, and you can easily understand how chip carving grew in popularity.

However, the evolution of these basic chip carving tools did not stop here. Listening to the concerns and suggestions from hundreds of my students, I introduced a set of three tools in the early 1990s that was designed to produce maximum results with either the traditional or the more contemporary styles of chip carving.

Look at **Figure 2-5** and examine the blade on knife 1. Notice how the radius has been reduced between the cutting edge and the back edge of the blade. The smaller radius means less metal in the wood while you are executing the cuts and, consequently, less chatter when you are carving curved chips. The handle was also made wider, giving the carver a greater, unobstructed viewing area in addition to providing a better grip. Knife 2 was added simply because the hands of a smaller person are smaller than those of larger carvers. While it may not seem like a big deal to many, having smaller tools can make a huge difference—just ask those with smaller hands! Other improvements to these U.S.-made knives include higher quality steel, reduced blade thickness, and precision grinding. These features mean that the knives will hold an edge well, will draw through the wood with less effort, and will require less sharpening time when brand new.

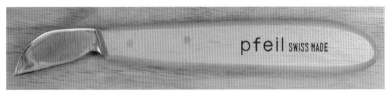

Figure 2-3. The Swiss eventually refined their approach to include only two basic tools—the cutting knife (1) and the stab knife (2).

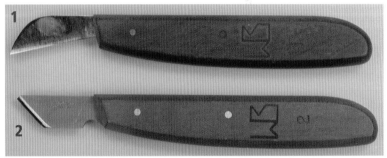

Figure 2-4. Notice the downward angle of the blade as it comes from the handle of the main cutting knife. This blade angle was a huge innovation that helps in maintaining the consistency and proper angle for carving.

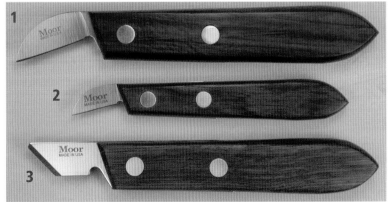

Figure 2-5. A set of three tools, introduced in the early 1990s, that was designed to produce maximum results with either the traditional or the more contemporary styles of chip carving.

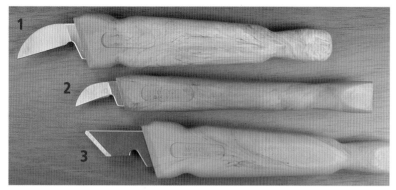

Figure 2-6. Improvements to the Moor chip carving knives included a longer handle for knife 2 as well as more ergonomically shaped handles for knives 1 and 3.

Chip Tip

Moor knives are available either "pre-sharpened" or "unsharpened." Whichever type you choose, you will need to keep them sharp. See Chapter Three: Sharpening for sharpening tips.

Figure 2-7. Notice how the ergonomic handle is designed for the proper grip.

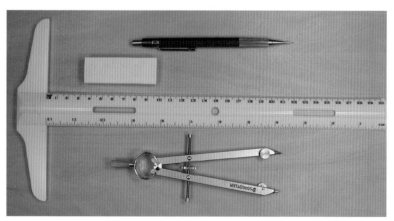

Figure 2-8. Basic drawing tools: 0.5mm mechanical pencil with B lead, white polymer eraser, 12" T-square, and 6" bow compass.

Today's Chip Carving Knives

The popularity of the original Moor knives did not mean there wasn't room for improvement. Chip carvers discovered that the new small cutting knife (knife 2) was just the ticket for making those intricate and delicate chips (See **Figure 2-6**.). While carvers with smaller hands were delighted, those with larger hands asked for a longer handle. I also worked with the manufacturer to design an ergonomically shaped handle for knife 1 that would include precise features for the carver's grip whether he or she is right- or left-handed (See **Figure 2-7**.).

Today's chip carving knives feature a textured finish, technically referred to as "a coefficient of friction," which means that they are easier to hold on to. The high-impact, synthetic handles are molded with interior fasteners, the blades are the same high-quality steel as the original Moor knives, and the knives continue to be made in the U.S.

DRAWING INSTRUMENTS

Chip carving is a fairly inexpensive carving style to practice due to the limited number of tools and drawing aids required. The new carver, therefore, is encouraged to purchase the best quality he or she can afford.

Basic Drawing Tools

A 0.5mm mechanical pencil with B lead for sharp and precise lines is a must (See **Figure 2-8**.). A 12" T-square that has both English or Imperial and metric markings is invaluable, as is a 6" bow compass. I use a white polymer eraser for removing or correcting pencil lines, and I buy them in bulk!

Chip Tip

A chip carver's toolbox should include:
• 1 or 2 cutting knives
• stab knife
• 0.5mm mechanical pencil with B lead
• 12" T-square with both English or Imperial and metric markings
• 6" bow compass
• white polymer eraser

Templates

Another helpful tool is a border layout template (See **Figure 2-9**.). It will save you a great deal of time when drawing borders' grids (See **Figure 2-10**.). Other templates (See **Figure 2-11** and **Figure 2-12**.) that you may wish to add to your collection at a later date include a six-inch/metric plastic ruler that is flexible, a protractor for dividing circles into various sections, a radius template, a flexible marking guide, and a circle template (also ellipse template).

SAFETY

One very pleasant fact about chip carving is that it is a very safe carving style. Because of the way you hold the knife and because your hand rests on the wood, you should never cut yourself. Should you hold the knife improperly, however, then the possibility of "adding color to your work" becomes very real. We will talk more about this in the Chapter Four: How to Hold Chip Carving Knives.

You'll also want to consider using a protective apron. Because we will be carving on our laps and not on a worktable, we'll need to protect our laps. Why do we carve on our laps? There are a couple of reasons.

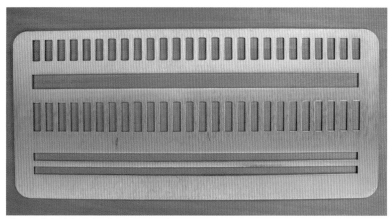

Figure 2-9. A border layout template.

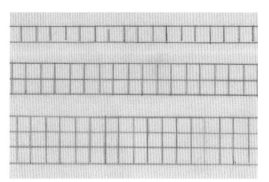

Figure 2-10. You will often use these basic grid lines in borders.

Chip Tip

Removing unwanted pencil lines once your carving is finished can be easier if you prepare the wood first. See page 78 in Chapter Fourteen: Finishing.

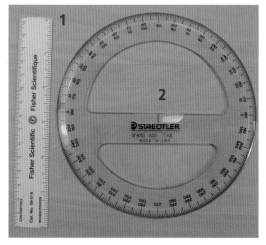

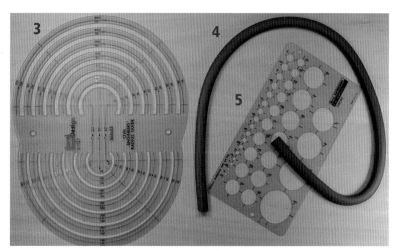

Figure 2-11 and Figure 2-12. Other useful templates that you might want to add to your tools: 1) a six-inch/metric plastic ruler, 2) a protractor, 3) a radius template, 4) a flexible marking guide, and 5) a circle template, or ellipse template.

Chip Tip

Holding your knife properly will help prevent the unfortunate experience of "adding color to your work" (mainly red)!

The first has to do with the position of our arms and how they bend at the elbow when we're carving on our laps. You will soon discover that it is much easier to chip carve using your upper arm/body strength rather than your wrists. Not only is it easier, but you can also carve for longer periods of time without fatigue. Bending your arms at the elbow allows you to make use of your upper arm/body strength easily. If you place your work on a table or bench, you cannot use your upper arm/body strength as easily.

Figure 2-14. Notice how the apron's work surface is reinforced with a heavy synthetic pad, protecting my leg or clothes from any stray cuts.

Second is the fact that consistent angles and chips are best obtained by holding your knife and workpiece in the same position all the time. Because chip carving is a very portable form of carving, you simply carry your knife and piece of wood with you, and then you can carve anywhere. Using different tables or benches at different locations would present a problem because they are seldom the same height as your work station at home. Your lap, on the other hand, is something you always have with you.

There are different devices you can use to protect yourself and your clothing while carving, such as a wooden tray or a leather apron. I use a leg apron (See **Figure 2-13**.) that was developed by the National Wood Carving School in Canada. It has a loop to hook onto your belt and three easy-snap straps to hold it in place. Because it bends at the knee, I can walk around or sit down while wearing it, and it isn't as warm as a full apron. The work surface of the apron is reinforced by a heavy synthetic pad, which will prevent any stray cuts from damaging your leg or trousers (See **Figure 2-14**.).

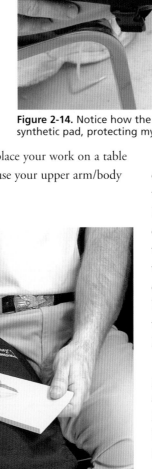

Figure 2-13. Because chip carvers often carve on their laps, they need to wear protective gear. Here, I am using a leg apron.

3

SHARPENING

If you are looking for sharpening instructions complete with technical data and high-power, microscopic photographs of tool edges, I am sorry to disappoint you. I have never been one to seek out (or provide) tons of detailed information that generally serves to confuse me as well as others. Should you simply want to know how to sharpen a chip carving knife, however, I believe I can help you.

Sharpening has proven to be a headache for many carvers. Over the years, I have discovered these five underlying reasons:

1) Too many experts giving too much data and insisting that theirs is the correct method.
2) The angle at which you sharpen your knife blade.
3) The motion you use when drawing your blade across the sharpening medium.

4) The sharpening medium you use.
5) The amount of time you spend on the process.

Let's look at each of the five reasons.

THE EXPERTS

First, do not get hung up on the technical data. If you really wish to know about aligning steel molecules, about various alloys and decarbs, and information that only a metallurgist really needs to know, then seek out that information from an appropriate source.

Second, don't be misled by those experts who insist that their method is the "correct and only way." There are numerous ways to sharpen a knife. If you have a system that works well for you, continue using it. The method I use works well for me and for hundreds of my students.

THE SHARPENING ANGLE

Different tools in your workshop require different sharpening angles, depending on their use. The blades in your joiner or thickness planer work best with a sharpened angle of 40 to 45 degrees (See **Figure 3-1**.). The edge on your beveled bench chisel works best at 30 to 35 degrees (See **Figure 3-2**.), while a mortise chisel is approximately 25 to 30 degrees (See **Figure 3-3**.). The edges on your carving knife, pocketknife, and even kitchen knives are optimum at 20 degrees.

All of the tools listed above are used to shave or peel wood away; that is, they remove small amounts of wood repeatedly until the desired results are reached. Chip carving cutting knives, on the other hand, are plunged directly into the wood and are pulled or drawn though it in a V-shaped fashion, resulting in a "chip" of wood

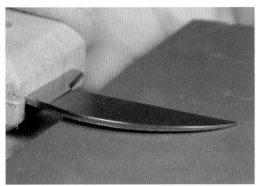
Figure 3-5. Ten degrees is about the thickness of the back edge of your knife.

popping out. Because of its use, the cutting knife works best when sharpened at an angle of 10 degrees or less (See **Figure 3-4**.).

To begin sharpening the cutting knife, hold the back edge of the knife blade approximately 10 degrees from the surface of the sharpening stone (See **Figure 3-5**.). Holding the blade at a steeper angle will mean more force is needed to both plunge and draw it through the wood.

The chip carving knife known as a stab knife is sharpened at a different angle. You will find sharpening instructions for the stab knife in The Sharpening Medium on page 13. I'll also offer comment on using power sharpeners later. For now, I am assuming that you are sharpening by hand.

THE MOTION YOU USE

There are lots of opinions on this topic. Some claim that you should draw the knife away from the cutting edge; others claim that you should push the knife toward the cutting edge; and still others suggest making a circular motion. I don't believe it makes any difference. The photographs on page 13 show my suggested method.

First, stroke the knife toward the cutting edge (See **Figure 3-6** to **Figure 3-8**.). Then, without removing the blade from the stone's surface or changing the angle, draw the knife back away from the cutting edge (See **Figure 3-9** and **Figure 3-10**.). This will give you a fairly steady, back-and-forth stroke that makes it easier to maintain the correct 10-degree angle as well as speeds up the process. Do not remove the knife from the stone's surface.

Figure 3-1. This joiner blade has an angle of approximately 45 degrees.

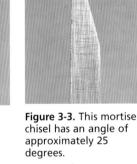
Figure 3-3. This mortise chisel has an angle of approximately 25 degrees.

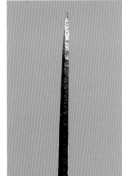
Figure 3-2. This bench chisel has an angle of approximately 35 degrees.

Figure 3-4. The angle for a chip carving knife, as seen when looking at the back edge of the blade.

Figure 3-6.

Figure 3-7.

Figure 3-8.

Figure 3-9.

Figure 3-10.

Chip Tip

Do not remove the knife from the sharpening stone. Simply move it back and forth while maintaining a 10-degree angle.

THE SHARPENING MEDIUM

I prefer to use ceramic sharpening stones for a few reasons. First, they will never wear and will always remain flat. Second, they do not require lubrication and therefore are clean to use. You will notice I said "ceramic sharpening stones," and not just "ceramic." Ceramic varies in degrees of hardness depending on its use. Ceramic floor or wall tiles are not the same as sharpening stones. In my experience, those who try ceramic stones soon discover their superiority and never return to other types.

Oil and water stones will wear and become very uneven. It is this wearing that explains the necessity for making them so thick. The average oilstone is at least 1¼" thick. Any thinner and the stone would be more difficult to use due to the uneven wearing.

If you use either oil or water stones for your gouges or narrow tools, you will soon discover a dishing, or hollowing, effect. Once this effect occurs, it is impossible to sharpen a flat-edged blade on the dished surface. While oil and water stones can be flattened or dressed, people seldom take the time or effort to do so. Both stones, as their names imply, must be lubricated for best results. Such lubrication is messy and cumbersome, especially if you happen to be carving in your living room (as I do) or outdoors under a shade tree (as I do) or while waiting for your spouse at the mall (also, as I do).

Diamond stones are an option, but only in part. Diamond stones are quite aggressive, and even the finest grit diamond stone is still too coarse, in my opinion. You can certainly use a medium or even a fine diamond stone to sharpen and shape your chip carving knives, but there is nothing like a superfine ceramic stone for fine honing just before stropping.

Sharpening is a three-step process—shaping the angle, fine honing, and stropping. I recommend ceramic sharpening stones that are approximately

Figure 3-11. The dark ceramic stone (left) is approximately 800-grit. The white ceramic stone (right) is approximately 8000-grit

2" x 4" in size for the shaping and fine honing. These stones are available in two grits: the dark ceramic stone is approximately equivalent to 800-grit, and the white one is approximately 8000-grit (See **Figure 3-11**.). The compact size allows them to be hand-held, which is important in maintaining that consistent angle I mentioned earlier.

Step One—Shaping

Use the dark, more aggressive ceramic sharpening stone to shape the blade to the 10-degree angle using the back-and-forth stroke described earlier. On a brand-new, unsharpened knife, this may well take you 10 minutes or 40 minutes, depending on the particular knife you purchase. Some chip carving knives come pre-sharpened (especially the more expensive, custom-made knives), while other mass-manufactured knives come unsharpened. The knives we are using are available both sharpened and unsharpened. Regardless of which chip carving knives you decide to purchase, you will have to sharpen them sooner or later, and it is very important that you learn the process right from the beginning.

Follow the instructions in The Motion You Use, page 12, and you will see the immediate results of your shaping process as metal begins to appear on

the surface of the sharpening stone. Pay close attention to this shading or metal residue because it will tell you if you are holding the knife correctly and if you are applying even pressure across the width of the stone.

How long this shaping process will take depends a great deal on how much pressure you apply. Using light pressure will, of course, take longer than using more force, but using too much pressure before you are experienced can quickly cause damage that may take a lot of effort to correct.

What kind of damage? Carefully watch the shading on the stone. If you have shading only at the tip of the knife blade, then you may not be holding the knife flat and therefore may be applying more pressure to the tip. More pressure on the tip of the blade can cause the tip to become round instead of pointed. If you have shading only at the heel of the knife blade, then you are applying more pressure to the heel than to the tip, causing the heel to shape improperly. When you first begin the shaping process on the darker stone, with the more aggressive grit, you may have shading at the tip and the heel, but no shading in the center portion. This is okay, as long as you have shading in more than one location. As you continue to shape the blade to the perfect 10-degree angle, the shading will become more and more even or consistent (See **Figure 3-12**.).

Step Two—Fine Honing

For fine honing, we switch over to the white ceramic stone, which at 8000-grit feels more like glass than a sharpening stone. Many people question how something so smooth can actually hone. Let me assure you that it does, and it does so superbly. The very fact that we see shading, which is really metal particles on the stone, is proof of the work the stone is doing.

This fine honing smoothes the shaping scores, or scratches and marks, as well as removes any burr that has developed. A burr is simply a very fine thread of metal that has not broken away from the edge. The shaping process develops this

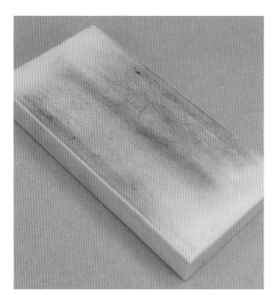

Figure 3-12. This photo shows the shading patterns you often see when you are shaping. The two darker lines on the left were made at the beginning of the process; then, as the sharpening progressed, the center area began to shade. The stone was then turned around, and the knife was sharpened on the other side of the ceramic stone when the shading became more and more even.

burr, which is often broken off without being noticed. If you do happen to notice a burr, it is nothing to become alarmed about because it is a natural occurrence in the sharpening process.

As you fine hone, you will notice the blade's cutting edge becoming more and more polished. When this polish or shine is consistent right across the blade's edge, you are ready for step three—stropping.

Step Three—Stropping

Using a good quality leather strop will polish the cutting edge to a mirrorlike finish (See **Figure 3-13**). Putting it simply—the more polished or shiny the cutting edge, the easier the knife can be drawn through the wood and the smoother your cuts will be. You cannot over-strop.

For hand stropping, I recommend a double-sided, heavy, 9-oz. leather strip glued to both sides of a 12-inch-long paddle board about 1¼" in width (See **Figure 3-14**.). On one side, have the rough side of the leather facing out; on the other side, have the smooth side of the leather facing out.

Apply a liberal amount of stropping compound to the rough side of the leather. If you wish, you can add a bit of fine oil (mineral oil, 3-In-One oil, honing oil, etc.) to the rough side to keep it supple. Leave the smooth side clean and without compound. There are several compounds available, and they are color-coded to show their different degrees of aggressiveness. Red offers an extremely fine grit, green offers a more aggressive grit, and white and gold compounds offer the most aggressive grit. All of these compounds are good; choose one based on your personal preference.

Keep your knife flat when moving it down the length of the strop. When you reach the end, lift it straight off without rolling your wrist or letting the blade go over the edge. Rolling your wrist or going past the strop's edge will cause the blade's edge to round over and lose its razor-like finish. Be sure to strop both sides of the blade.

A common question is "How often should I sharpen?" Once you achieve the optimum cutting edge on your knife, you will be aware when it requires a touch-up. Signs might include your using more effort to draw the blade through the wood, your cuts not being as smooth, or the blade just not feeling "right." When you notice any of these, it is time to freshen the edge. I generally find that my chip carving knife requires

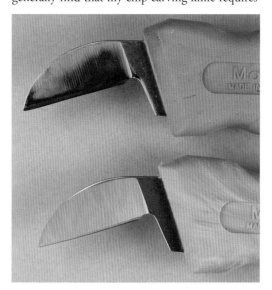

Figure 3-13. Compare the polished edge of the top blade to the unpolished bottom blade.

Chip Tip

Because chip carving knives are sharpened on both sides, they work equally well for left- or right-handed carvers. They are also held in the same manner, which we will cover in Chapter Four: How to Hold Chip Carving Knives.

Chip Tip

The more you strop, the easier the knife will draw through the wood and the smoother your cuts will be.

Figure 3-14. Be sure to keep your knife flat when stropping.

just a stropping after about every two or three hours of carving. It can vary depending upon a variety of factors, such as the type of wood you are working with and how perfect the edge was to start. Let me also suggest that about every half-dozen times you strop, you fine hone on the white ceramic stone for a couple of minutes and then strop. After about every half-dozen times you use the white ceramic stone, go all the way back to the dark ceramic stone, then use the white stone, and then strop.

Sharpening the Stab Knife

The stab knife is sharpened at a different angle because of its use. Instead of being used to remove wood, the stab knife is merely pushed or "stabbed" into the wood, resulting in the wood fibers being separated in the shape of the blade. It has an edge angle of approximately 25 degrees, similar to that of the mortise chisel shown earlier. Unlike a cutting knife, it is not the stab knife's bevel or angle that is crucial but rather the actual width of the blade.

Notice that the tip of the stab knife is not ground to a point, but to an angle. This angle permits it to penetrate the wood easier as well as leave a nice "square back" to the impression it creates (See **Figure 3-15**.). **Figure 3-16** shows the

Chip Tip

Remember, sharpening is a three-step process. Each time you use the dark stone, you must then use the white stone and then the strop.

25-degree angle to which the stab knife is sharpened. As with the cutting knife, sharpening the stab knife is a three-step process: first use the 800-grit stone, then the 8000-grit stone, and then the leather strop.

How Can You Tell When the Knives Are Sharp?

I see all kinds of methods for testing sharpness, including the following: shaving the hair from the back of your hand or wrist; holding the blade at an angle and touching it to your thumbnail, using little or no pressure, to see if it will grip without sliding off; and slicing a piece of paper. Here is an original thought: Why not try it on a piece of wood?

The knives should cut crisply, cleanly, and with little pressure, leaving no marks or fuzzies. If you feel that the knife sticks or drags, it needs more attention. In fact, if you are having difficulties or problems, 85% of the time it is because of the knife's not being sharpened properly and stropped to perfection. If you are positive that the knife is fine, but your cuts are not as clean or as crisp as they should be, especially on cross-grained cuts, then the problem may be with your

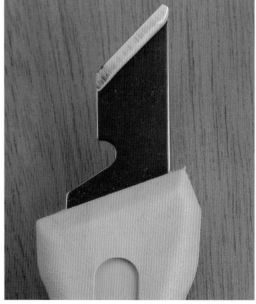

Figure 3-15. The tip of the stab knife is ground to an angle rather than to a point.

Figure 3-16. The stab knife, sharpened to a 25-degree angle. This stab knife comes in a pre-ground state and requires only minimal sharpening.

wood. Remember that wood carves best when it has an approximate moisture content of 10%. If it's less than 10%, you may even hear the wood cracking as you cut.

THE AMOUNT OF TIME YOU SPEND ON THE PROCESS

This just might be the biggest reason for those who have difficulty sharpening. We stop just before we have reached the perfect edge, much like the time we take to shake an aerosol can of spray finish. The directions on the cans always read the same regardless of the brand: "Shake can for one minute before using." I believe that, for most of us, one minute is closer to ten seconds. Mixing the contents of an aerosol can by shaking it is just about as exciting as watching paint dry, and it takes a lot more patience than I generally have. But, taking the time to mix the paint correctly improves the final result, just like taking the time to properly sharpen your knife makes the quality of your work better. So, take your time and be sure to complete the sharpening process. It may take a little longer when you first prepare your new knife, but once you have that perfect edge, it won't take much to maintain it.

Power Sharpeners

If you are a brand-new carver, and especially a knife carver, I do not recommend that you rush right out to purchase a power sharpener. Learn to sharpen by hand; you will never regret it.

If, however, you are a woodworker or wood-carver who needs a power sharpener for your other tools as well as your knives, that is a different story. Power sharpeners are available in all sorts of sizes, styles, and price ranges. I have seen and used some that cost hundreds of dollars, and even a couple that cost thousands of dollars, but I have never found a better power sharpener than a simple, converted, 1" belt sander. Power sharpeners that use wheels mounted vertically are okay for gouges and chisels, but it is pretty tough to sharpen a knife or plane blade on a wheel. The horizontal wheels solve the problem but are very expensive for the average carver or woodworker.

The belt sander (See **Figure 3-17.**) should have the belt running away from the operator, not toward the operator, for safety reasons. Many motors can be rewired to accomplish this reverse polarity without much difficulty. The ideal speed for this type of sharpener is around 1300 rpm. Go much faster than this, and the chance of burning the tool and therefore losing the temper, or hardness, is very real. Leather belts are also available for these machines and make stropping a breeze.

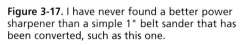

Figure 3-17. I have never found a better power sharpener than a simple 1" belt sander that has been converted, such as this one.

HOW TO HOLD THE KNIVES

You might not think that how you hold your knife is a big deal. You would be wrong! A big part of the attractiveness of chip carving is the shadows that are created and the consistency of the angles of the cuts. Of course, the designs or motifs are very important, but even the greatest of designs may turn out less-than-great if carved poorly. We can accomplish the consistency of angles in two ways: 1) by always working in the same physical position and 2) by holding the knives in exactly the same manner and position on each and every project.

Remember, by carving on our lap, or at least with our arms bent at the elbow as described in Chapter Two: The Tools (see page 6), we will have a consistent physical position wherever we carve.

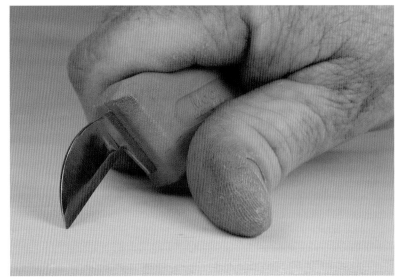

Holding your chip carving knives properly is essential to creating attractive finished pieces.

THE ANGLE OF THE CUTS

The angle of your cuts will determine the effectiveness of the shadows and the overall appearance of your carving. You know by now that in order to remove a chip of wood, you must make at least two cuts. Both cuts are made at an angle, facing each other, to create a V shape.

It is the angle of the V that makes all the difference in the world. Cuts made at 45 degrees, the incorrect angle, permit light to roll into the chips, whereas cuts made at 65 degrees, the correct angle, show a sharp line where the light stops and the shadow begins. The natural tendency is to make the cuts at too low of an angle. This tendency is quite understandable because making a V-shaped cut at a 45-degree angle means that you do not have to go as deep into the wood before your cuts will meet at the bottom. If you make the cuts at a 65-degree angle, you will have to go much deeper into the wood before your cuts will meet (See **Figure 4-1** to **Figure 4-4**.).

HOLDING POSITION FOR THE LARGE KNIFE: POSITION ONE

Now that you understand the importance of making cuts at a 65-degree angle, how can you be guaranteed of consistent results? The answer's simple—hold the knife in exactly the same position all of the time. This is quite easy to accomplish.

Look at the large knife in **Figure 4-5**, and you will see that it has two indents in the handle. On the top edge of the handle, there is a finger indent, in which you place your "Peter Pointer," or index finger. **Figure 4-6** shows the position with the finger resting in the finger indent and on the wood that is being carved. Close to the blade and across from the finger indent is the thumb indent. **Figure 4-7** shows the position with the thumb resting in the thumb indent and on the wood that is being carved. Go ahead and try holding the knife this way while looking at these photographs. This position is known as position one. Because there are only two positions, you have already accomplished 50% of the technique!

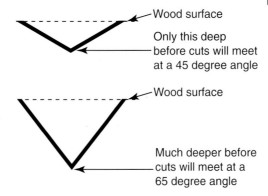

Figure 4-1. Notice how much deeper the 65-degree cuts must be to meet than the 45-degree cuts.

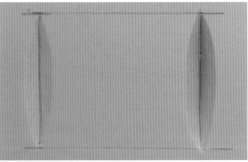

Figure 4-2. Shown here are actual cuts in a basswood board. The cut on the left was cut at 45 degrees; the cut on the right was cut at 65 degrees. You can see a remarkable difference in the shadows cast by the two cuts. These are simple one-chip examples—imagine the effect in a complete, chip-carved project.

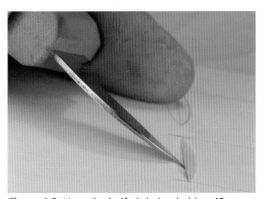

Figure 4-3. Here the knife is being held at 45 degrees—the incorrect position.

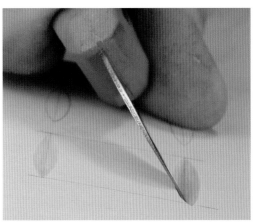

Figure 4-4. The knife is held at 65 degrees—the correct position.

Chip Tip

The angle of your cuts will determine the effectiveness of the shadows and overall appearance of your carving. In fact, the difference in shadows between cuts at a 45-degree angle and cuts at a 65-degree angle is quite unbelievable.

Now check to see if you are holding the knife so the blade will cut at the proper 65-degree angle. Figure 4-4 shows a front view of the proper angle. An important note: If, when you first check your grip, you discover that you are not holding the knife at the proper 65-degree angle, do not twist your wrist or hand to achieve the 65-degree angle. Twisting your wrist or hand will create an unnatural position for you. If you are not holding the knife properly, simply loosen your grip and turn the knife within your hand until it rests at the 65-degree angle. Now tighten your grip.

By always holding the knife in this position, you will assure yourself of consistent, correct angles. Also, remember to keep your finger and thumb in contact with the wood at all times. This contact is not only part of the correct position, but it is also part of the reason that it is

just about impossible to cut yourself. As you make your cuts, your hold will move and, because your hand is moving with the knife, safety is automatic. Should you be tempted to remove your thumb from the knife handle and plant it firmly on the wood to use for leverage—*don't.* If your knife slips, you will add color to your wood: namely, red!

HOLDING POSITION FOR THE LARGE KNIFE: POSITION TWO

Though you will use position one for 95% of your cuts, there is a position two, which will come in very handy. Position two involves holding the knife with the blade facing the opposite direction that it faces in position one. That is, the cutting edge faces away from your thumb and person, rather than toward your thumb and person (See **Figure 4-8**.).

Notice that, in position two, your thumb is placed on the back edge of the knife as well as on the handle. Keep your fingers in contact with the wood at all times for support and stability. **Figure 4-9** illustrates how your fingers should rest on the wood.

It is more difficult to hold the knife at a 65-degree angle consistently using position two because you do not have the natural jig that came with holding both your finger and thumb on the wood as you did for position one. With a little practice, you will see that position two really isn't hard to learn.

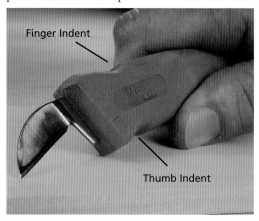

Figure 4-5. The ergonomic handle provides finger and thumb indents for proper grip.

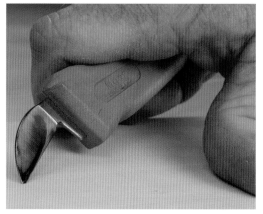

Figure 4-6. Notice how the finger also rests on the wood while you carve.

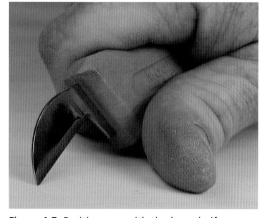

Figure 4-7. Position one with the large knife. Notice that the thumb also rests on the wood.

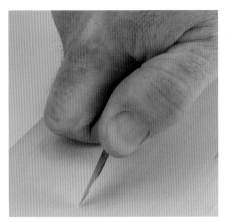

Figure 4-8. Position two with the large knife.

Figure 4-9. Notice how the thumb is placed on the back edge of the knife and on the handle. Keep your fingers in contact with the wood at all times.

Figure 4-10. Notice how the handle flares out for added grip.

Figure 4-11. The handle of the small knife is long enough to protrude past your grip.

Figure 4-12. Hold the small knife at a 65-degree angle just as you would the large knife.

Chip Tip

Left-handed? Not to worry, simply hold the knife in your left hand in exactly the same manner. Remember, the knife blade has been sharpened on both sides and works equally well with either hand.

So when will you use this position? I can think of three occasions when position two is good to know. First, use position two to prevent splitting. Sometimes, when you are cutting with the grain and using position one, the wood may want to split ahead of your knife, similar to what happens when you split wood for the fireplace. If you feel the wood begin to split, *stop.* Switch over to position two and cut back into your already-executed, position-one cut.

Second, use position two to make the second cut of the triangle chip. You will very soon begin making triangle-shaped chips from the instruction in this book. We will discuss why we use position two for the second cut when we reach Chapter Five: Three Main Shapes of Chip Carving.

Third, use position two in confined areas. There will be times when you are chip carving within a confined area, such as on the inside, along the side, or along the end of a box. Position two will be very useful for these situations. You won't use it a lot, but you will be glad you know the technique.

HOLDING POSITIONS FOR THE SMALL KNIFE

Holding the smaller knife isn't any different than holding the large knife, except that there are no indents to guide you. The small handle does have a peculiar shape, however, and is designed to help those with large hands as well as those with smaller hands.

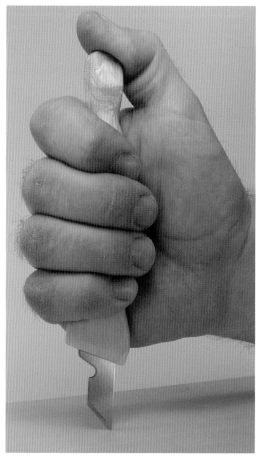

Figure 4-13. Holding the stab knife with the blade in an outward position.

Figure 4-14. Holding the stab knife with the blade in an inward position.

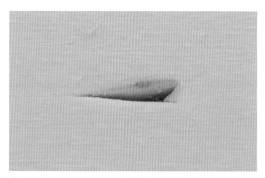

Figure 4-15. A single stab knife impression.

Figure 4-10 illustrates how the center of the handle flares out in width. You will find that this shape has a natural feel in your hand and provides an ergonomic grip. Figure 4-11 shows the long handle and how it actually protrudes from your grip. The added length is certainly beneficial for those with larger hands who wish

to use the smaller blade for more intricate cuts. Figure 4-12 illustrates the proper holding position and the 65-degree angle, covered previously in the large knife demonstration. Position two for the small knife is accomplished in the same way as it is with the large knife (See Figure 4-8 and Figure 4-9.).

HOLDING POSITION FOR THE STAB KNIFE

This knife gets its name from the job it does and from the manner in which it is held. It is such a simple knife, and it performs such a simple task that many underestimate its importance. Let's first learn how to hold it. **Figure 4-13** shows the stab knife being held with the blade in an outward position. **Figure 4-14** shows it being held with the blade in an inward position. You

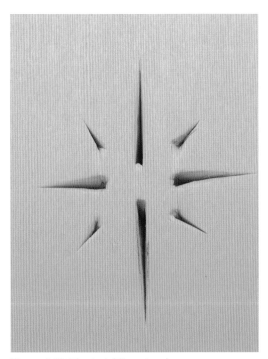

Figure 4-16. The twinkling-star shape.

can hold it either way, depending on the impression (meaning a score or groove in the wood, rather than a feeling you are trying to portray) you want to create. Actually, you can hold the blade in any direction you wish: inward, outward, sideways—it is really up to you.

Now stab, or plunge, the knife into the wood. No, do not take aim with the knife in the air and actually thrust it into the wood (you may miss and hit your leg). Simply position the point on the wood and push it in. The width of the blade of the stab knife and the manner in which it is sharpened will cause an impression in the wood as illustrated in **Figure 4-15**.

If you are not very impressed with my impression, you are not alone. Many feel this way. Yet, as I suggested earlier, do not underestimate its importance. For example, when you are working with grids or embellishments, you may want to add a small design, such as a twinkling-star shape (See **Figure 4-16**.). You can do these designs quickly and easily with simple impressions. Imagine the floral design in **Figure 4-17** without the stab marks. See the difference?

Figure 4-17. Notice how simple impressions enhance this floral design.

The thickness of the blade separates the wood fibers far enough so that they will not fill in completely when you add a finish. However, they will shrink somewhat depending on their size.

5
THREE MAIN CHIP SHAPES

It may seem hard to believe, but chip carving is made up of only three main shapes. When you first see a chip carving, it may appear complex and difficult to carve because of the many shapes and sizes of chips within the overall design. However, if you break the design down into individual chips, you will discover only three main shapes: the two-sided, or curved, chip; the three-sided, or triangle, chip; and the straight-line chip.

THE TWO-SIDED, OR CURVED, CHIP

This chip is the easiest to carve because it has only two sides. It also has the greatest number of variations and shapes (See **Figure 5-1**.). To carve it, simply hold your cutting knife (either the large or small knife) in position one and draw it along one side of the chip at the 65-degree angle learned earlier. Then, remove the knife from the

Figure 5-1. This group of flowers is almost entirely made up of two-sided chips. The exceptions are the stab marks and a couple of petals. Can you find them?

wood, turn the board around 180 degrees, and carve the other side of the chip in the same manner (See **Figure 5-2** and **Figure 5-3**.). Go ahead and try a few of the two-sided chips on page 26 (See **Figure 5-4**.). For the exercises we'll be doing, you'll want to have a practice board. Ideally, the board should measure ⅜" x 4" x 12".

So you made your first attempt at chip carving, and the chip didn't just pop right out, eh? ("Eh" is the Canadian way of saying "huh.") Well, don't be too disappointed; it happens all the time. The reason is simply that you did not cut deep enough for the two 65-degree cuts to meet and release the chip. There could be a number of different causes:

• The chip is too large for you.
• Cross-grained cuts are more difficult than cuts made with the grain.
• You didn't use enough strength.
• You just do not have enough strength.
• Your knife isn't sharp enough and hasn't been stropped enough.
• It's your first attempt.

You will be happy to know that whatever the reason, there is a remedy for it.

Figure 5-5 shows my practice board with two rows of two-sided chips. In **#2** on the top row, a 65-degree angle cut has been made on both sides. First, the cut was made on side **A**; then the board was turned around 180 degrees, and the cut was made on side **B**. The chip is still there, isn't it? In **#3**, the chip was cut again on both sides at what was thought to be exactly the same angle. The chip did pop out this time—perhaps "break out" would be a better description. The actual results look a lot like the cuts were made by a beaver with a loose tooth. The last example in the top row shows the cleanup attempt. The chip was cut again at the same angle to remove all signs that it was poorly done in the first place. There were three attempts to remove this chip, and even then it still doesn't look great. I have no problem relating that this exercise resembles many of my first attempts at chip carving. The remedy to this progression is simple: don't try to remove the chip with only two cuts.

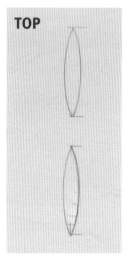

Figure 5-2. A simple curved, or two-sided, chip. To carve it, simply hold the cutting knife in position one at a 65-degree angle. Cut into the wood along one side.

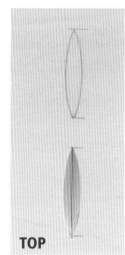

Figure 5-3. Then, remove the knife from the wood, turn the board around 180 degrees, and carve the second side in the same manner.

Chip Tip

Remember—we carve on our laps, so please use a safety apron or similar item for safety's sake.

Chip Tip

Cut, don't pry. Resist the temptation to pry out a stubborn chip for two reasons. First, the chip will break off instead of being cut off, and the result will be a messy-looking carving. Second, you may damage your knife. Basswood is fairly light in weight, but don't be fooled into thinking it isn't strong. The knife that you have taken time to sharpen and polish comes to a very fine point, and prying the wood may just leave you with a broken tip.

The second row shows that a small chip was removed from inside the larger design. By making this smaller chip, we have made a void where the wood can move to when we attempt the second and final cuts. Making the first cut was easy because it is small. Making the second, larger cut was also easy because it basically removed the same amount of wood as the first cut did. And, note how clean the final result is.

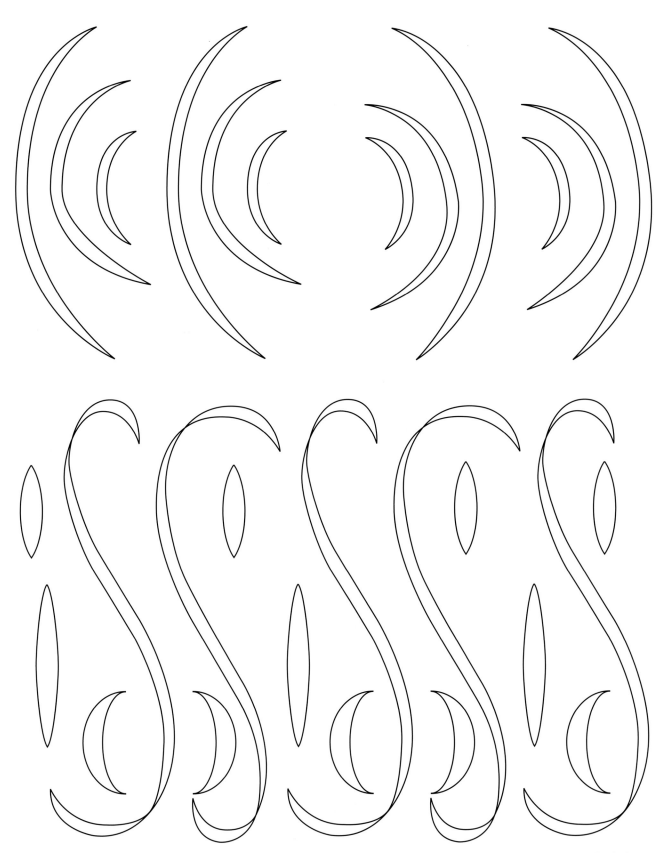

Figure 5-4. Practice Exercise. The patterns shown here offer a good variety without too much of a challenge right away This little exercise will help you to become familiar with your knife and with how the wood reacts to your cuts. Try some chips with the grain and some across the grain. Use basswood for best results. Remember, this is just practice.

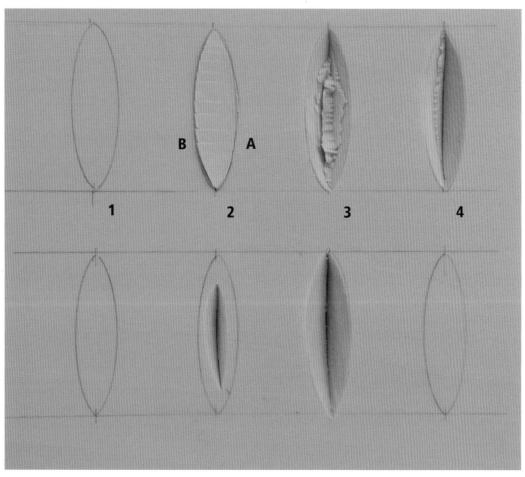

Figure 5-5. The top row of the practice board shows an attempt at removing the entire chip at once. The second row was done by taking out a smaller chip first.

Chip Tip

If the chip doesn't "pop out," then you haven't gone deep enough with one of your cuts. If this happens to you, try the next pattern of the same size, but first remove a smaller chip within the larger chip—see the photo and instruction at the left.

You don't have to be Superman to make large chips; simply start with smaller chips in the center and work your way outward.

When viewers first examine a beautifully chip-carved piece, they often ask how we are able to make the cuts on both sides of a chip meet exactly at the right depth to enable the chip to come out. Oh, if that exactness were really possible! But nobody, absolutely nobody, can do that. What we can do is make sure the second cut surpasses the depth of the first cut. Some call this technique an undercut; some call it an over-cut. It really doesn't make any difference what you call it, as long as you make sure the cut is deeper than it has to be.

Okay, I know your next comment: "Then why can't I see the undercut in the finished result? The chips look perfect to me." The answer is simple. The cut has closed up after the chip was made. Let me compare it to when you cut your finger. (Here I mean the type of cut that isn't serious and that certainly does not require stitching-up by the doctor.) A simple bandage will stop the bleeding, and it will heal rather quickly. We all have done this. Look now at where those cuts were on your finger. They have completely healed without any scars or telltale marks. Should your cut have been serious and have required a doctor's attention and stitching-up, there would be a scar. An undercut in carving works the same way. If it isn't too serious (meaning much deeper than really necessary), the wood fibers will close back up. If they do not close by themselves, they will when you apply your first coat of finish because the wood will soak up the finish, closing the cuts nicely.

THE THREE-SIDED, OR TRIANGLE, CHIP

Carving this chip is a little more difficult than carving the two-sided chip because the triangle chip has one more side. The most common place to find three-sided chips is in the borders carved to frame a project. Certainly, you will find three-sided chips within rosettes as well as in free-form motifs, but generally not in the same abundance as in borders. We will begin carving borders made entirely of three-sided chips in Chapter Six: Standard-Sized Borders, so let's take a few minutes to learn how to make these chips. The first set of drawings (See **Figure 5-6** to **Figure 5-8**.) illustrates the basic grid or outline for a typical three-sided chip. These are not to scale. The step-by-step demonstration (See **Figure 5-9** to **Figure 5-14.**) captures the process for making the cuts.

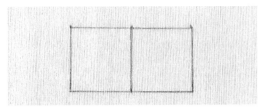

Figure 5-6. The basic grid is two squares drawn side by side.

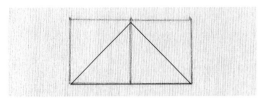

Figure 5-7. Draw a triangle within the two squares.

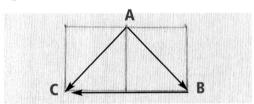

Figure 5-8. Make the first cut from point A to point B while holding the knife in position one. Make the second cut from point A to point C while holding the knife in position two. Turn the board on your lap until you are comfortable. Make the third cut from point B to point C while holding the knife in position one. Turn the board again until you are comfortable.

CARVING THREE-SIDED CHIPS

Figure 5-9. Make the first cut holding the knife in position one. The thumb and finger are on the board.

Figure 5-10. A close-up view of the first cut.

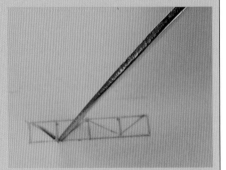

Figure 5-11. Make the second cut holding the knife in position two. This position is shown in Figure 4-8 and Figure 4-9 on page 21.

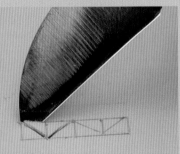

Figure 5-12. Make the third cut holding the knife in position one. Again, the thumb and finger are on the board.

Figure 5-13. As you make the third cut, draw your knife across the line to complete the cut.

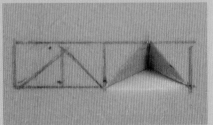

Figure 5-14. A close-up view of the completed three-sided chip.

LAYOUT AND MEASUREMENTS FOR THREE-SIDED CHIPS

As mentioned earlier, the ideal size for a practice board is ⅜" x 4" x 12" and, of course, basswood is the absolute best wood to use. You can draw these grids directly on the board using a 12" T-square and a 0.5mm mechanical pencil with B lead. You can also use a border layout template as described in Chapter Two: The Tools. Don't draw the lines right to the edge of the board because it is dangerous at this stage to carve too close to the edge.

I am offering most of the measurements in metric and suggest that, although it might be a bit of a nuisance for you at first, it will definitely be to your advantage later. Metric is much easier to use for layouts because it is based on tenths, unlike the English or Imperial system which has no standard increment. Most 12" T-squares are available with both English or Imperial and metric measurements (See **Figure 5-16** in the Chip Tip.) Then why do we call it a 12" T-square? Because if they were called 30cm T-squares, most of us would respond with "Huh, what's that?" ("Huh" is the American way of saying "Eh.")

Now that you are ready, get to it! Practice and see what happens (See **Figure 5-15**.). One more suggestion first: carve each triangle one at a time. Resist the temptation to make all of the first cuts across the whole row, followed by all of the second cuts, and then the third cuts. This way, if you do have some trouble, you will be able to see the problem quickly and remedy it without repeating the error on each and every chip. Once you see that the chips are popping out nicely, by all means go for the repeated first, second, and third cuts. As a matter of fact, you will find that you will become more consistent in your angles when you begin to do repetitive cuts across the whole row.

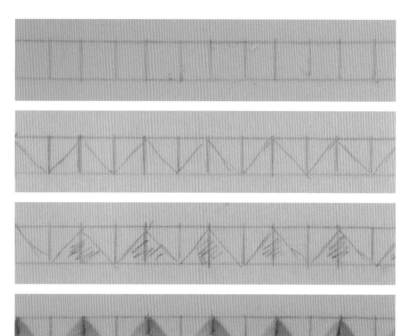

Figure 5-15. For this grid, each square is 4mm x 4mm. First, draw the horizontal lines while marking the 4mm spaces. Then, using the T-square, mark the vertical lines. Next, draw the diagonal lines—you can just do these freehand. You may find it advantageous to shade in the triangles you plan to chip out, as I have done in the third row.

Chip Tip

A quick metric lesson. Figure 5-16 has been enlarged for easy viewing. Note the marks at 1, 2, 3, 4, etc. These marks represent centimeters. Each of the ten small marks between each centimeter represents a millimeter. There are ten millimeters in each centimeter.

Most of the measurements I will offer, especially in laying out borders, will be in metric. Learning this system now would be a good idea.

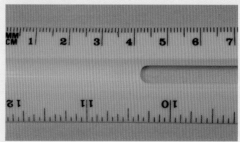

Figure 5-16. Many rulers and T-squares have both English or Imperial and metric measurements. This one has been enlarged to show detail.

Chip Tip

Practice this three-sided triangle cut over and over and over again—literally hundreds of times. It's the most difficult cut to perfect, but repeating the cut will give you the skills necessary to perform the curved and straight cuts with ease.

HAVING PROBLEMS?

Let's look at some common problems that you may find yourself experiencing (See **Figure 5-17**.).

Run-off

If your last cut, or third cut, continually runs off the line as you draw your knife across the two squares, it will probably help if you hold your elbow closer to your body.

Curled edge

Curled edges are caused by pushing your knife too deeply into the wood when you first start your third cut. It will take a bit of practice to perfect, but don't dismay. To fix the curled edge, simply place the blade of your knife back on the first cut and undo the curl. It may look like you are going to trim the curled edge, but you will find that the curl will actually tuck back down and leave a smooth-looking cut.

Beaver tooth

Ah, the old loose-beaver-tooth effect. This effect occurs especially in the very bottom of the chip. If you are seeing a beaver tooth in a cut, you are not cutting deep enough. Lay your knife back into each cut, making sure it is at the same angle, and finish the cut to the proper depth. Make sure the point of your knife has not become rounded over from incorrect sharpening.

THE STRAIGHT-LINE CHIP

The straight-line chip is mainly used for borders or for framing-in your work. I like to compare a chip-carved border around your work to a picture frame around a painting or wall hanging. The purpose of the frame is to keep your eyes within a confined area so that your eyes are focused on the work itself and not distracted by the surroundings. You would never purchase a painting or print and hang it without a frame. Nor should you leave your carved design unframed or without a border.

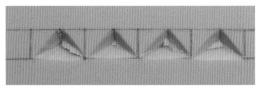

Figure 5-17. Three common problems that chip carvers may experience: run-off (top), curled edge (middle), beaver tooth (bottom).

Look at **Figure 5-18** and **Figure 5-19**. They are both the same positive diamond carving, except that a simple straight-line chip has been added to and the gridlines have been erased from Figure 5-19. Quite a difference. (See Chapter Six: Standard-Sized Borders, page 32, for more information on the positive diamond carving.)

Carving a straight-line chip is done by holding the knife in position one and carving at a 65-degree angle along one side of the chip. Then, turn your board and carve back along the other side. To remove the chip, you will have to make tiny stop cuts at each end of the chip. It is a very simple technique, and yet look at the difference it makes.

Figure 5-18. A positive diamond carving without straight-line chips.

Figure 5-19. A positive diamond carving with straight-line chips.

You should be able to get a pretty straight line with a little practice, especially for lines that are only three or four inches long. What about straight lines that are longer than three or four inches? These lines can present a problem because you have to shift your arm and/or the carving at some time or another to reach all the way to the end. Try this method that seems to work fine for me (See **Figure 5-20**.). Use a razor blade (the type for which you break off a dull portion to expose a new edge) and score the wood along the line very lightly. Just score the surface; do not cut into the wood very deeply at all. Use a steel ruler to guide the razor blade (See **Figure 5-21**.); then use your chip carving knife and follow the score of the razor blade, keeping that 65-degree angle, of course. You will be surprised at how your knife will follow the score almost perfectly.

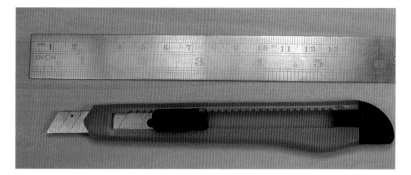

Figure 5-21. A steel ruler and a razor blade for cutting long straight-line chips.

Chip Tip

Remember to score the wood very lightly with the razor blade—do not cut very deep. If you cut too deeply, you will notice a secondary, jagged edge once you remove the chip using the proper 65-degree angle.

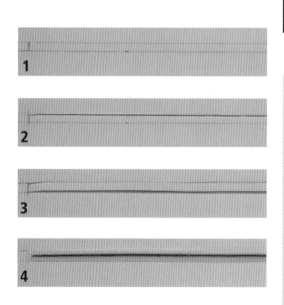

Figure 5-20.

1: A straight line drawn to a width of 2mm. The width of your straight lines will vary depending on the actual size of your project.

2: Score one side using a razor blade and a steel ruler. Then, cut the line, holding your knife in position one.

3: Score the second side and cut in the same manner after turning the board 180 degrees.

4: Make the stop cuts at each end, and the long chip should pop out.

Tips for Carving a Straight Line

• Twist your wrist outward so that the blade in your knife is in a straight line through your knife, your hand, and up to your elbow. Then, lock your wrist in this position. Holding your knife this way will help to stop your knife from wandering as you follow the pre-drawn line.

• Hold your elbow close to your body. This too will help to keep your knife from wandering. You may have to practice a little before you get the hang of it.

• Try to keep your eyes focused on the line about half an inch ahead of the knife blade. When driving your car, you don't look at the hood; rather you look down the road in the direction you are headed. This same concept works for carving straight lines. Again, you will have to practice a little before you get it perfect.

6

STANDARD-SIZED BORDERS

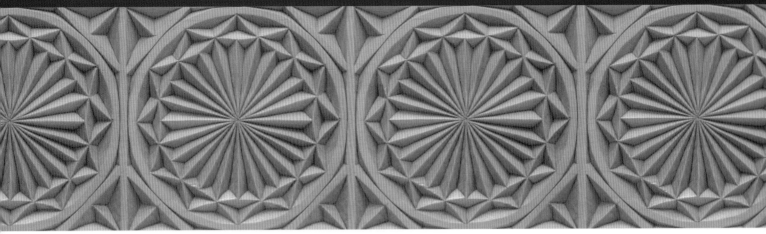

I talked about the importance of borders in the previous chapter, Chapter Five: Three Main Shapes of Chip Carving, so let's get down to making a few of them. The exercises in this chapter should be done on basswood practice boards 4" wide x 12" long x ⅜" thick. First, we will carve some using the three-sided, or triangle, chips, which you should have perfected by now. Then, we will make some using two-sided, or curved, chips. The variety of borders is virtually endless, and I would encourage you to eventually develop some of your own designs.

So what do I call a "standard-sized border"? A standard-sized border would be used to decorate projects about the size of an average jewelry box or smaller. By average, I mean one that might be found on my wife's dresser, not a princess's.

STANDARD-SIZED BORDERS USING THREE-SIDED CHIPS

Let's make a border. Begin with the basic grid of 4mm squares, as shown in #1, using either a T-square or a border template (See **Figure 6-1**.). Draw these grids across the grain of your practice board. #2 shows diagonal lines drawn freehand to form the three-sided chips. Note the shading of the chips to be removed. #3 shows a complete row of three-sided chips. If your project is a very small box or plaque, this border just might be sufficient itself. #4 shows a grid with a double row of 4mm squares. You can see how confusing this might be as you determine what chips you should remove. Shading will help to eliminate some of the confusion, at least until you become familiar with the patterns. #5 and #6 show two different chip selections and illustrate how different the carved border can appear depending on the chips selected.

Perform these three-sided cuts in the sequence and holding positions offered in Chapter Five: Three Main Shapes of Chip Carving. Make the first cut in position one, the second cut in position two, and the third cut in position one again. Turn the board when making the different cuts. The first and second cuts are so short that your hand should not move on the board. Simply position the knife so the point is in the correct place (at the top of the triangle), and then plunge it into the wood until the cutting edge of the blade touches the corner on the bottom line. When making the third cut, you will have to plunge your knife lightly into the wood and then deeper as you draw the blade across the length of the triangle.

I suggest you practice these steps in the order they are offered; then practice some more, and then some more.

Figure 6-2 shows our second set of borders. #1 and #2 are more variations using the double-grid row of 4mm squares.

We refer to #1 as a positive diamond because the diamond shape remains on the surface of the board while the background is chipped out.

We refer to #2 as a negative diamond because the diamond shape is cut into the wood, and the background is left on the surface. We could make a negative diamond with only four cuts, but it isn't nearly as attractive as making it with two three-sided chips. The two three-sided chips leave a sharp ridge on the surface and therefore create another shadow.

The #3 border illustrates an embellishment to the #1 border. The addition of very small, two-sided, wedge-shaped cuts to each side of the positive diamond is very easy and quite fast, yet it makes a remarkable difference. Why? It adds more shadows, and that's what it is all about. I like to call these little cuts my "politician cuts." I have found that politicians in just about every country have the uncanny ability to flip-flop on their campaign promises once elected to office. To make these cuts, you first flip your knife using position one and then flop your knife over to position two for the second cut

(See **Figure 6-3** and **Figure 6-4**.). Start each cut with the cutting edge at the end of the diamond and finish the cut in the center. Be sure to cut all the way into the center.

The #4 border shows an embellishment to the #2 border. Simple, little three-sided chips in between each negative diamond give the border a whole new appearance. I like to call this one "adding the ooohhs."

Sometimes it is difficult to know when to stop carving a pattern and call it finished. There always seems to be another embellishment that we could use to enhance the final appearance. I generally let the price of a commission decide when enough is enough. If it is a gift, then I guess it depends on how much the recipient means to me.

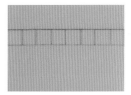
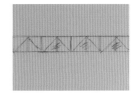
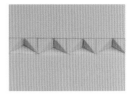
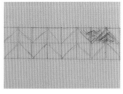
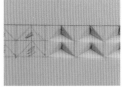
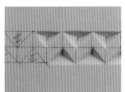

Figure 6-1. Basic border practice. Each square in the grids is 4mm in size. Leave a 5mm space on each end. Notice in the fourth row that I have shaded one upside-down and one right-side-up triangle. You can remove either, depending on the pattern you want to create. The pattern in the sixth row is called a chervon.

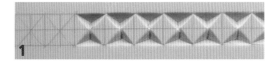
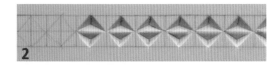

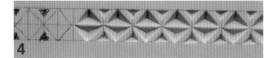

Figure 6-2. Four more border variations. Be sure to leave a 5mm space on each end.

Chip Tip

At this point, it doesn't matter if you flip first or flop first when making the small, two-sided cuts. Later it will, because sometimes, if you flip before you flop, then the flip that you are trying to flop will cause the flop to flip, and the whole flipping flip will be a flop.

Here are more borders using the simple, three-sided chip (See **Figure 6-5**.). Consider the top row of chips for a moment and watch how the appearance changes when we merely point the triangles in a downward position as shown in **Figure 6-6**.

Just in case you were wondering, the 4mm measurements being used are not my idea. These measurements have been used for centuries, and I believe they were developed for two reasons: ease of execution and appearance. Even when we look at larger borders in the next chapter, you will see that we still use the 4mm base.

STANDARD-SIZED BORDERS USING TWO-SIDED CHIPS

As attractive as the preceding borders are, they are not suitable for all projects. Perhaps I should say that there could be more suitable borders, depending on the project and the recipient. Because the three-sided chips are geometric, they lend themselves very nicely to rosettes and geometrically shaped centerpieces. For projects using a free-form motif, you may want to consider borders using two-sided, or curved, chips. For instance, if you are making a keepsake box for someone who loves horses or dogs, a border with a rope design would be much more suitable than a diamond pattern.

To make a rope border, first draw a double row of 4mm squares (See **Figure 6-7**.). Second, use a template to draw the arcs. Notice that the arcs span two 4mm squares on the top and bottom. Third, draw the diagonal lines freehand. Notice how they exactly intersect the corners of the squares. **Figure 6-8** shows a section of a completed rope pattern that has been carved in butternut and stained.

Next, let's look at making a petal border (See **Figure 6-9**.). First, make two 4mm-wide horizontal rows. Second, draw vertical lines 15mm apart. Third, use a template to draw arcs. Notice that the arcs span two vertical lines, and the bottom arcs create overlapping lines. To finish the petal shape, use half of the template shown in **Figure 6-10**.

Figure 6-3. First flip...

Figure 6-4. Then flop.

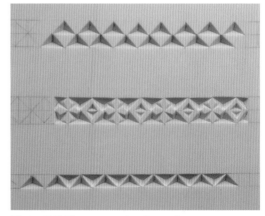

Figure 6-5. Three more borders using three-sided chips.

Now that we have our pattern established, we can start carving. Make the first cut, A, while holding the knife in position one (See **Figure 6-11**.). Turn the board around 180 degrees and make the second cut, B, while also holding the knife in position one.

Notice in **Figure 6-12** that the blade is facing away from the first chip removed. The cut began at A and ended at B. If it had begun at B, the chance of breaking out the small area of wood that separates the two curved chips would have been very high.

Finish carving each petal across the border. You will see in **Figure 6-13** that I have added a three-sided chip in between each of the petals. These are drawn freehand, and I attempted to follow the contour of the petal rather than drawing a simple straight-line triangle. Because these triangles have curved lines, we will carve them using position one for all three cuts. Doing so will present a problem, but it's a problem that we can easily solve.

Figure 6-13 shows that when we hold the knife in position one, the tip of the blade does not meet the apex of the triangle as does the cutting edge further up the blade. Therefore, when the cutting edge reaches the apex, it is necessary to stand the knife up by bringing the point up to meet the apex as shown in **Figure 6-14**. Remember to keep your thumb on the board. Do not remove the knife from the wood; simply stand the knife up all in the same cutting motion. Now, remove the knife from the first cut, turn the board, and make the second cut also using position one (See **Figure 6-15**.). You will see that the tip of the knife should now meet the first cut you made (See **Figure 6-16**.). Complete the chip by turning the board again and making the third cut also using position one.

Figure 6-6. If you use this border on a project, you will discover that when the triangles point outward, the project will appear to be larger than when the triangles point inward.

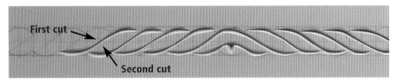

First cut

Second cut

Figure 6-7. Creating a rope border. Use a template to draw the arcs in the top row. Draw the diagonal lines and inside arcs freehand. Shading is optional, but it's always a good idea to do a few.

Figure 6-8. A section of rope border carved in butternut and stained.

Chip Tip

Figure 6-10. You'd be surprised at the types of things that make great templates.

Templates come in all sorts of shapes and sizes. This is one that I personally use quite a bit (See Figure 6-10.). Many people confuse it with a washer, but, of course, it is not a washer. Washers are purchased for their inner diameter. Templates, on the other hand, are purchased for their outer diameter. You may purchase a template from the same store that sells washers. In fact, washers and templates are very close to the same price, even though templates are much more valuable. The template shown has an outside diameter of 1⅜", or 35mm, or 3.5cm. It's a good one!

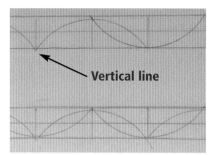

Figure 6-9. Creating a petal border. Notice how the arcs span two vertical lines.

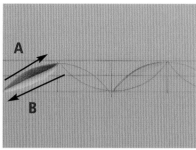

Figure 6-11. Make the first cut, A, while holding the knife in position one. Turn the board 180 degrees and make cut B, holding the knife in position one. Be sure to leave a 5mm space on each end.

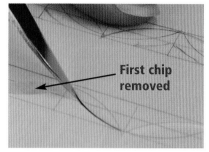

Figure 6-12. Notice how the blade is facing away from the first chip removed. Cutting away from the previously removed chip will help to prevent breakout between the chips.

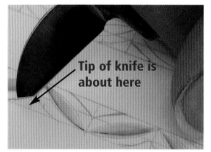

Figure 6-13. The cutting edge has reached the apex.

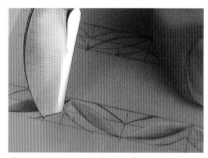

Figure 6-14. Stand the knife up so that the tip reaches the apex.

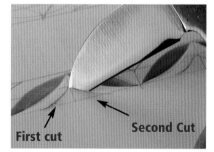

Figure 6-15. Make the second cut.

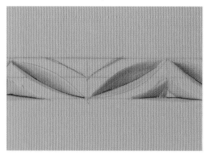

Figure 6-16. If the knife is stood up correctly, the cut will look like the cut on the left. If the cuts do not meet correctly, the result will look like the chip on the right.

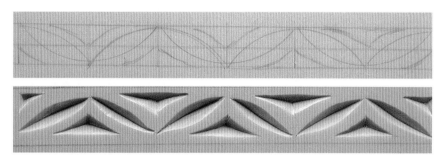

Figure 6-17. The completed border.

Chip Tip

Remember to make a smaller chip within the larger chip if you find it too difficult to carve in one attempt.

Figure 6-17 shows the completed border. Notice how the triangular chips are carved in the corners. You will run into design challenges at times, and we will cover some solutions in Chapter Eleven: Layout and Design.

Though this next set of curved-line borders has the appearance of lace, the borders are certainly not fragile whatsoever (See **Figure 6-18**.). As such, they lend themselves well to projects that might be handled often, and you can feel confident that the carving will not be damaged through normal use.

The first pattern needs no explanation and is pretty straightforward to draw and to carve. I used the 1⅜" washer/template shown on page 35 to make the arcs. I told you this template's a good one!

The second pattern requires a little more thought and time to draw. It begins with the standard two 4mm-wide horizontal rows. I have added two additional horizontal lines approximately 1.5mm to 2mm inside the outside lines.

The vertical lines are only 1cm apart. Use a smaller circle template to draw the arcs. Refer to the photo when you are drawing the pattern, and you should not have too much difficulty in getting it perfect. This is also a pretty hardy border even though it has a delicate appearance. It also lends itself well to staining—we will talk about staining and finishing later on in the book in Chapter Fourteen: Finishing.

Choosing the correct border for your project is very important. Just like carving a rope border for an animal theme, here is an example of how the first border in this set takes on the appearance of waves when used with a dolphin (See **Figure 6-19**.). I think you will agree that while the second border takes a little more time to draw, it is well worth the effort. **Figure 6-20** shows the finished example.

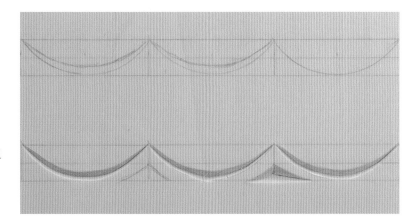

Figure 6-18. A set of two borders using two- and three-sided chips.

Figure 6-19. The border looks like waves when paired with the dolphin.

Figure 6-20. Though this border takes a bit more time, the finished product is well worth the effort.

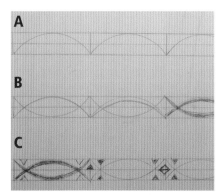

Figure 6-21. The drawing and layout of the Ing motif.

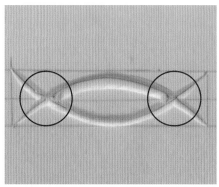

Figure 6-22. If you carve this design using only the 65-degree angle, you will get big-time chip-outs.

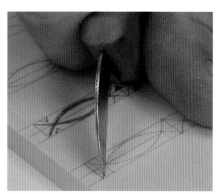

Figure 6-23. Start with your knife at almost 90 degrees to the wood.

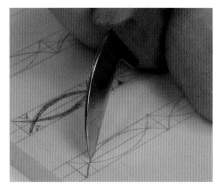

Figure 6-24. Cut shallow until you get through the intersection where the lines cross.

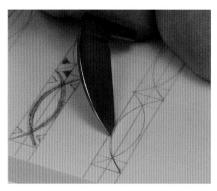

Figure 6-25. Once you get into the center area, lower your blade to a 65-degree angle.

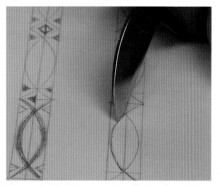

Figure 6-26. Raise your knife back to 90 degrees as you approach the next intersection.

The "Ing" Motif

The "Ing" motif has been around for centuries and is commonly found in Gothic ornamentation. It has a very delicate appearance when carved and is very suitable for borders on boxes that feature a rosette as the centerpiece.

Begin by drawing two 4mm rows horizontally across the width of your practice board (See **Figure 6-21**.). Then, add vertical lines 3cm apart. Just a note: a 4"-wide practice board is 10cm in metric. Because we will draw three sections of 3cm each, we have a drawing totaling 9cm wide. By leaving a 0.5cm (or 5mm) space at each end, the pattern will be centered on the board.

Draw three arcs as shown in line A. Can you guess which (washer) template I used? Then, draw three more arcs within the same confines as shown in B. These arc lines are the ones that we will carve. Rather than carving the arc lines as first drawn, let's make them a little wider in the center but bring them back to a point at each end. This inside arc can easily be drawn freehand and then shaded in if you wish. After carving the arcs, we will embellish the motif with small

triangular chips as shown in line C, but do not draw them just yet. You will see why in a minute.

It's time to start breaking rules. If you carve this design using only the 65-degree angle that has been drilled into you so far, you will have trouble. Look at the highlighted areas in **Figure 6-22**, and you will see exactly what will happen—big-time chip-outs.

To fix the problem of chip-outs, start with your knife at almost 90 degrees to the wood (See **Figure 6-23**.) and cut shallow (the chip is not very wide here) until you get through the intersection where the lines cross (See **Figure 6-24**.). Once you get into the center area, lower your blade to a 65-degree angle (See **Figure 6-25**.), but be prepared to raise your knife back to 90 degrees as you approach the next intersection as shown in **Figure 6-26**.

To complete the chip, turn the board and make your second cut in the usual manner—the usual manner being holding the knife in position one and at a 65-degree angle.

Once you have finished carving the three arcs, it is time to add the little three-sided triangle chips. If you had drawn in the small triangles and aligned them with the intersection where the arcs cross, you would now see that the alignment is wrong (See **Figure 6-27.**).

FRAMING WITH STRAIGHT-LINE CHIPS

I spoke of the importance of using a straight-line chip in the previous chapter and offered some tips and suggestions for carving it. When you are carving any of the standard-sized borders in this chapter, you will find that adding simple straight-line chips that are about 1.5mm to 2mm wide to both sides of the border will make a huge difference. Just look at the completed Ing motif border in **Figure 6-29.** It would not look nearly as attractive without the straight-line chips.

A few things to remember when framing borders with straight-line chips:
- The first line should be 2mm away from the original 4mm-wide rows (See **Figure 6-28.**).
- Remember the rule learned earlier: When making the first cut in a new chip, the knife blade should face away from the previous chip. This rule is very important when carving a straight-line border as well. Cut the first line first because your knife will be facing away from the border pattern. If you cut the second line first, the knife will be facing the border pattern, and the possibility of breaking out the wood between the line and the border pattern is very real.

Figure 6-27. If you had drawn in the small triangles and aligned them with the intersection where the arcs cross, the alignment would be off.

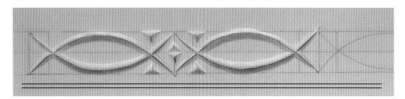

Figure 6-28. Laying out the Ing motif with a frame of straight-line chips.

Figure 6-29. A completed Ing motif border framed by straight-line chips.

Below is a summary of the standard-sized border patterns that we discussed in this chapter. Each of them employs the 4mm grid and the three-sided chip. Use these shaded patterns to aid you as you are learning to draw your own borders.

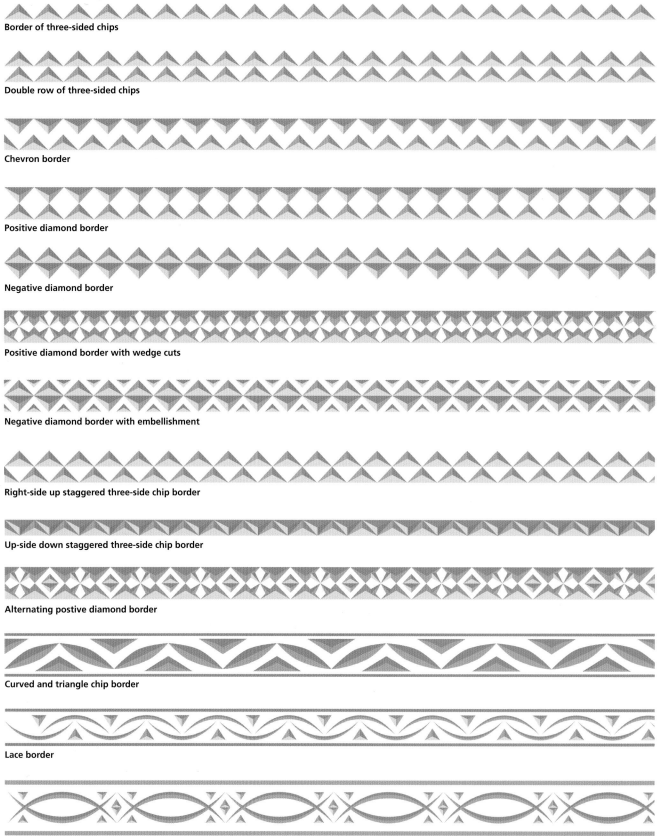

Border of three-sided chips

Double row of three-sided chips

Chevron border

Positive diamond border

Negative diamond border

Positive diamond border with wedge cuts

Negative diamond border with embellishment

Right-side up staggered three-side chip border

Up-side down staggered three-side chip border

Alternating postive diamond border

Curved and triangle chip border

Lace border

Ing motif border

LARGE-WIDTH BORDERS

In Chapter Six: Standard-Sized Borders, you will recall me mentioning (unless of course you didn't read all of my words of wit and wisdom) that the standard measurement of 4mm in borders is very

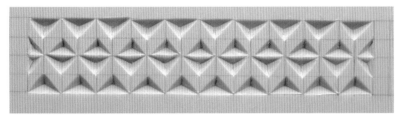

Figure 7-1. A double row of chevrons.

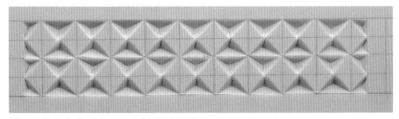

Figure 7-2. A double row of positive diamonds.

old and time proven. So, what happens when your project dwarfs those little 4mm squares? You may be tempted to increase the triangular chips to perhaps 6mm or 8mm or even larger. Doing so could be a mistake. While we will have to look at each project on its own, a general rule is that if you need a large-width border, you should keep the same 4mm-sized lines but increase the number of them. For instance, if you are carving the top of a box and one row of diamonds looks too small, don't increase their size, simply add another row.

These first five examples illustrate that, just as in Chapter Six: Standard-Sized Borders, each square is only 4mm in size; however, now there are four horizontal rows instead of two. This first example is a double row of chevrons (See **Figure 7-1**.). It's interesting to note that when you carve this pattern, you also create a row of

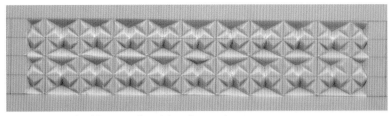

Figure 7-3. A double row of positive diamonds with flip-flop cuts on the side of each positive diamond.

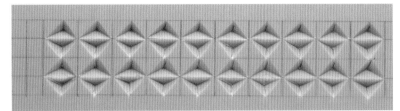

Figure 7-4. A double row of negative diamonds.

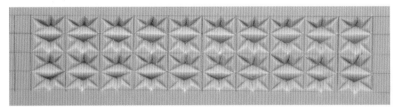

Figure 7-5. A double row of negative diamonds with flip-flop cuts on the side of the center row of positive diamonds and on the half diamonds.

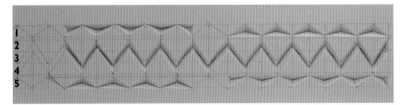

Figure 7-6. A wolf tooth border pattern. Each section is 6mm in width and 4mm in height. Note the 1mm space between rows 1 and 2 and between rows 4 and 5.

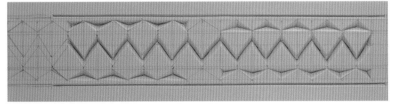

Figure 7-7. The wolf tooth pattern framed by straight-line chips.

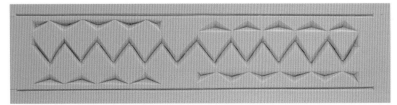

Figure 7-8. All of the reference lines have been removed.

negative diamonds across the center. **Figure 7-2** shows a double row of positive diamonds. Again, we have automatically created a row of negative diamonds along the center. **Figure 7-3** is the same as Figure 7-2, except that it has flip-flop cuts on the side of each positive diamond. You should remember these from Chapter Six: Standard-Sized Borders. **Figure 7-4** is a double row of negative diamonds. This time, we have created a row of positive diamonds across the center—completely unintentional, but attractive. **Figure 7-5** is the same as Figure 7-4 with the addition of flip-flop cuts on the side of the center row of positive diamonds and on the half diamonds. Sometimes it's hard to stop—or know when to.

The pattern in **Figure 7-6** is quite an old pattern called a wolf tooth. It is necessary to make each section 6mm wide, while keeping the 4mm height to get this appearance. **Figure 7-7** shows the same wolf tooth pattern with straight lines added to frame it. Notice the different effects achieved by carving the triangular chips pointing inward versus outward on the outside of the pattern. The carving in **Figure 7-8** has had all of the reference lines removed. Quite a difference, isn't it!

Next, we'll look at a popular design that will begin to challenge your skills. This pattern can be found in examples of Renaissance architecture. It is the unification of St. Andrew's cross and a four-sided rosette.

First, let's draw it (See **Figure 7-9**.). Begin with four horizontal rows of 4mm squares. I find it a benefit to darken the group of four center squares. For the arcs representing the petals of a four-sided rosette, use that washer/template you were introduced to back in Chapter Six: Standard-Sized Borders. You will notice that I have carved one section out already. Sometimes it can be confusing as to where you should begin the cuts, so I have put in points A, B, C, and D to help. All of these cuts are made holding the knife in position one. Begin at point A and draw your knife to point B. Then cut B to C, then C to D, and then from D back to A. Did the chip pop right out for you? Proceed to the next chip as shown in **Figure 7-10** and **Figure 7-11**.

We are now ready to move on to the next step. Check out **Figure 7-12**. Notice that I have added some darker lines between the petals and have assigned points A, B, C, and D. Before you begin the cuts, check out the chip that I have removed so that you have an idea of what we are after.

Hold your knife in position one. Actually, I am not going to remind you about position one any more because you should be well aware of it by now. I will only mention knife position when it is necessary. Begin your cut at point A and cut to point B. Do you know why? Remember that rule: "The first cut in the new chip should always be facing away from the previous chip." What do you think the next cut should be? B to C? How about C to A? Because B to C is a cut across the grain, I would personally choose C to A first and then cut from B to C to finally remove the chip (See **Figure 7-13**.).

Once those chips are carved, it is time to add the flip-flops in the center squares (See **Figure 7-14**.). Remember when to flip first or flop first so that you don't break off the points of the squares. The flip-flop cuts should all meet in the center of the square.

Figure 7-15 to **Figure 7-19** show some different examples of large-width borders.

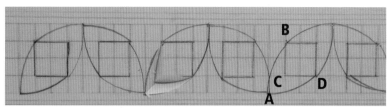

Figure 7-9. The pattern shown here is a combination of St. Andrew's cross and a four-sided rosette. Use the template to draw in the arcs. Leave 2mm of space and draw in straight lines 2mm apart. Then darken the center squares.

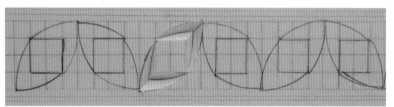

Figure 7-10. Finish the first set of cuts.

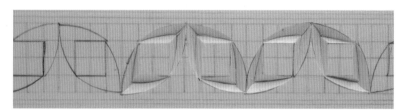

Figure 7-11. Keep moving along the row.

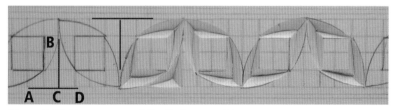

Figure 7-12. I have removed the first corner chip.

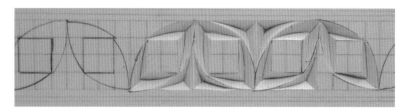

Figure 7-13. I continue making the corner cuts. Notice that I stop before the cuts become too delicate.

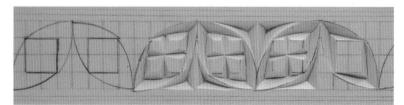

Figure 7-14. Here I've added in some of the flip-flop cuts.

Figure 7-15. An example of a completed Renaissance border pattern that has been lightly stained.

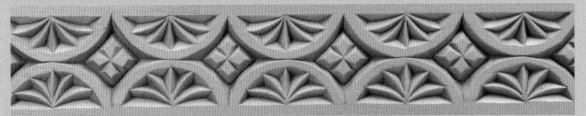

Figure 7-16. This border is close to full size and resembles a series of half wagon wheels.

Figure 7-17. This pattern would make not only a great-looking drawerfront, but also a wide border.

Figure 7-18. The pinwheel rosettes on the ends of this pattern are a challenge to carve. Practice them on a practice board first.

Figure 7-19. Shown here is a classic Renaissance pattern found throughout period architecture. This pattern was carved on the sides of a box, while the pattern in Figure 7-15 was used as a border on the top.

CURVED BORDERS

8

Up to this point, our borders have been designed for square or rectangular projects. While these shapes are the most common, there will be occasions when you will need a border for a round or oval project. A decorative or commemorative plate or perhaps a door plaque would be examples of projects for which we need to rethink the border layout.

Pictured in **Figure 8-1** is a 12"-diameter basswood plate. Notice the scalloped edge, which offers a decorative touch, and the rim around the recessed center. One of the most common borders for this style of plate is one that incorporates the scalloped-edge design into the border. To draw this border on your practice board, use a good quality bow compass to draw the two arcs. I discourage you from using the inexpensive type that holds a common pencil to draw. Your compass should have a mechanical adjustment

for opening and closing. (See Chapter Two: The Tools, where I cover the drawing tools.)

Figure 8-1. This 12"-diameter plate with a scalloped edge is a perfect candidate for a curved border.

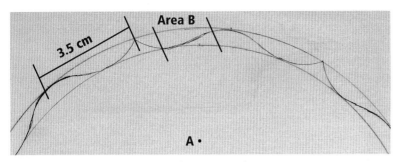

Figure 8-2. The completed pattern for our curved border.

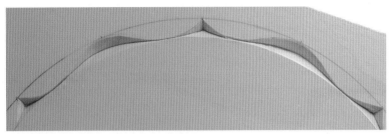

Figure 8-3. An easy, yet impressive, way to carve the design.

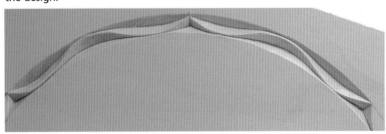

Figure 8-4. Carving both sides of the design gives a delicate effect.

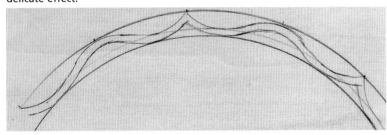

Figure 8-5. You can modify the pattern slightly by adding a second inner arc.

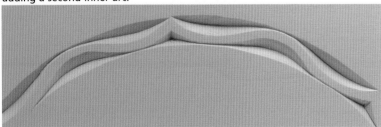

Figure 8-6. The pattern from Figure 8-5, carved on both sides.

Place your compass point in a random spot, A, and open it to a radius of approximately 8.5mm to draw the outer arc. Now, reduce the radius by 6mm and draw the inner arc. It is important that these arcs are only 6mm apart. Next, mark off every 3.5cm around the outside arc as indicated in **Figure 8-2**.

The next step is to draw the scalloped line. Notice that the design has a repeating point-hump-point-hump pattern. Just in case you haven't guessed by now, there is a tool you should already have in your possession that is perfect for drawing the points and humps. Yes, the washer/template! You will have to draw in the area between the point and hump freehand (See area B in Figure 8-2.), but, with the main radius established, you should not find that too difficult.

Figure 8-3 shows one way to carve the design. It is rather easy, yet impressive, and would show up nicely if stained. I will talk about staining later in Chapter Fourteen: Finishing.

You could also carve both sides of the line for a beautiful and very delicate effect (See **Figure 8-4**.). This carving would be excellent for a clear finish, but would not be suitable for staining.

Here is an alternative way to carve basically the same pattern. Use the exact same drawing instructions, except this time make the inner arc very faint (See **Figure 8-5**.). Draw a second inner arc that is 8mm inward from the outer arc. Once you have drawn the points and humps, just like in the first drawing, draw a second line 2mm away from the first. When you carve this one, leave the 2mm-wide rib (See **Figure 8-6**.). This pattern provides a much less delicate carving that would be excellent for a clear or stained finish.

A curved border of triangles is another good border to have in your arsenal (See **Figure 8-7**.). Draw it by using your bow compass to draw two arcs 6mm apart (See **Figure 8-8**.). Now, mark every 4mm along the inside arc. When you are making these marks, don't be concerned that your ruler doesn't bend with the arcs. Just make about four or five of the marks, and then move your ruler along and mark another set of four or five.

They will not be 100% accurate, but they will certainly be close enough that the human eye cannot tell the difference. To mark the points on the outer arc, align a 6" ruler with the compass hole and one of the 4mm marks. Now mark on the outer point. No need to mark every 4mm, just every other one.

Also try a curved crescent border (See **Figure 8-9** and **Figure 8-10**.). Use your washer/template to draw the crescents. These two arcs are only 4mm apart. Take a look at **Figure 8-11** to **Figure 8-18** for more border ideas.

Chip Tip

Sometimes it is necessary to anchor the pattern so that it doesn't appear to be floating. Look at the horse in Figure 8-18. Because of his trotting pose, it is necessary to add the ground. Without the ground, or anchoring, the horse would appear to be floating in midair. The rope border ties in nicely with the theme.

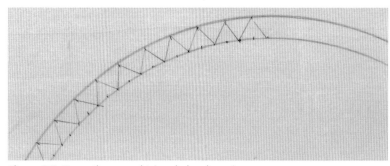

Figure 8-7. Draw the curved triangle border using a bow compass and a ruler.

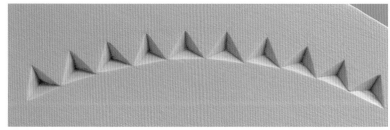

Figure 8-8. The finished curved triangle border. Pretty simple, isn't it? And yet, pretty impressive when done on a project.

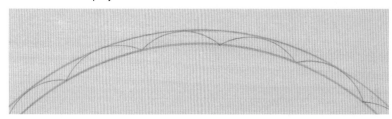

Figure 8-9. Use your washer/template to draw the crescent border.

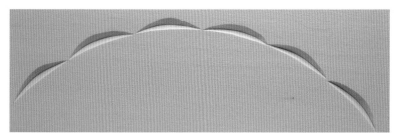

Figure 8-10. The carved crescent border.

Figure 8-12. Borders do not always have to be geometric in shape. Nor does the same pattern have to repeat all the way around.

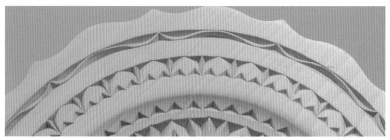

Figure 8-11. A combination of three curved borders. The center one is called an egg and dart, which is commonly found in Swiss and other Western European carvings.

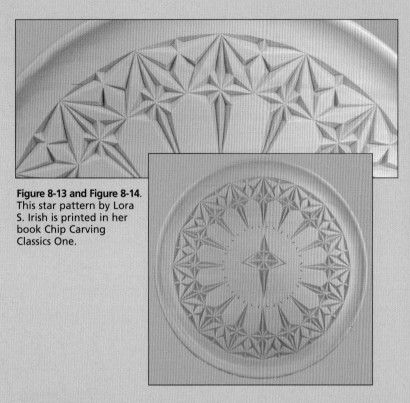

Figure 8-13 and Figure 8-14. This star pattern by Lora S. Irish is printed in her book Chip Carving Classics One.

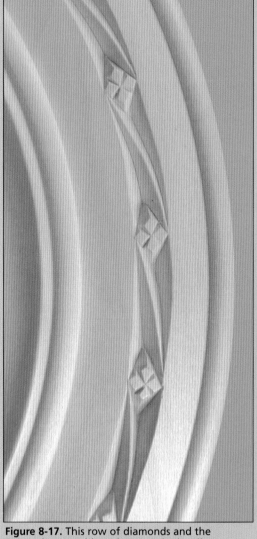

Figure 8-17. This row of diamonds and the Santa plate would not have worked well together because the themes do not tie in.

Figure 8-15 and Figure 8-16. While the border does not have to be geometric nor repeated, it must have the same theme as the project. The Santa plate and the poinsettia leaves and berries go well together. In case you are wondering, that is color you see in the foliage. It's just like me to tempt you with staining; I will talk about it later in the book in Chapter Fourteen: Finishing.

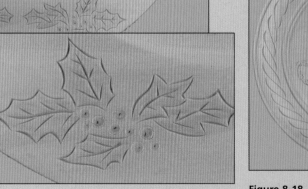

Figure 8-18. The addition of ground keeps the horse from floating in midair.

These two borders come from the same basic pattern. The line pattern will provide a good starting point for your drawing; the shaded patterns are to aid you as you get ready to carve.

9
GRIDS

Grid motifs present an option for a variety of projects. First of all, they present an overall pattern that can solve layout and design problems for projects with a large area to cover. Serving trays, door panels, entire box tops, and chests are examples of large areas where grids could work nicely. Grids can also be used as a background for a central theme or motif.

I believe you will find that diamond-shaped or circular grids are more appealing than square or rectangular ones. Diamond shapes of 60 degrees present a great pattern for your grid, and they are quite easy to draw.

Begin by drawing a rectangular frame that has a length approximately one and a half times as long as its width. Examples would be 4" x 6" or 6" x 9", which is great because most boxes or plaques use the same principal. After drawing the rectangular frame, divide the width and the length into the same number of sections.

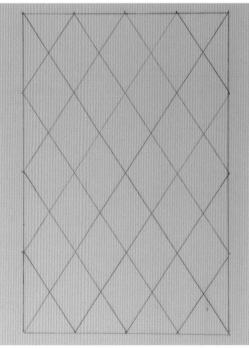

Figure 9-1. Our practice grid, shown here, is 8cm in width and 12cm in length. Both the length and width have been divided into four sections.

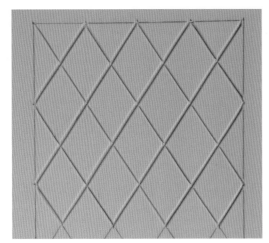

Figure 9-2. This grid is a simple straight-line pattern.

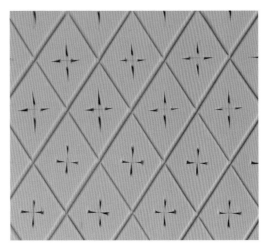

Figure 9-3. A stab knife was used to create the impressions in the centers of the diamonds.

Let's use **Figure 9-1** as our practice grid. First draw a frame 8cm wide (note cm, not mm, or approximately 3⅛") and 12cm long. Divide both the length and the width into four sections, which creates 2cm-wide sections across the width and 3cm sections along the length. Make sure that you are just marking these sections and not drawing lines completely across or down the frame you have created. Now, use a ruler to draw diagonal lines to divide the sections. I like to use a 6" ruler for this task.

The first exercise using this grid is a simple straight-line pattern shown in **Figure 9-2**. While this is pretty simple, it can be rather impressive on a project. Simplicity is the beauty of chip carving, eh!

> **Before you begin:** If you had drawn this pattern on an actual project instead of a practice board, you should carve the outside lines of the frame first. By carving the perimeter lines first, the diagonal line chips you carve will pop out.
>
> In Figure 9-2, I only carved the diagonal lines and therefore had to put in little stop cuts at the end of each chip. Choose which method you like.

Once you have finished carving all of the diagonal lines (and have admired your work), let's add a few of those "ooohhs." "Ooohhs" are the sound you will hear when people look at your work and see that you have taken an extra minute or two to dress it up. Use your stab knife to make impressions in the center of each diamond (See **Figure 9-3**.).

Chip Tip

Take a good look at Figure 9-3 again. Notice that the stab impressions across the bottom two rows are different than those in the top two rows. Using the stab knife with the point outward makes quite a different pattern than using it with the point inward.

For the next exercise, use the same grid layout, but this time add some crescent shapes to each of the sections as shown in **Figure 9-4**. Just in case you have *no idea* what to use to draw the crescents, may I be so bold as to suggest using your washer/template.

My suggestion for the order of cuts for beginners would be to start with A. Make all four of the inside cuts on that diamond first; then make all of the outside cuts to remove the chips. Move on to B, but make the outside cuts first this time to follow the rule that for "the first cut

Chip Tip

Try to carve off your drawn lines to save cleanup time later. To do so, it might be necessary to draw the crescents slightly smaller than you want the finished shape to be.

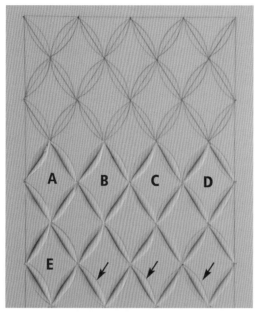

Figure 9-4. Use your washer/template to add crescent shapes to the diamonds.

in the new chip, the knife blade should face away from the previous cut." After you have completed C and D, move to the next line and begin E.

If you find that your chips are coming out cleanly and without any re-cutting, you may wish to try a faster approach. Cut all of the " ⤢ " lines across the row first; then go back and remove the chips. Choose the next row to your liking, and so on.

Take a good look at your grid. Pretty nice looking, isn't it? You should be proud of it. Sometimes, I have found that holding the carving at arm's length will make it look better. Other times, a distance of five or six feet between you and the carving helps even more. I recall one

student asking me to hold his carving while he stepped back about ten feet or more. He exclaimed, "It sure looks good from afar, but it's far from looking good!"

Let's add a couple of "ooohhs." **Figure 9-5** shows where I have carved some flip-flops in every other row. Notice how the cuts meet in the center. **Figure 9-6** shows where I have carved flip-flops on each diamond or portion thereof.

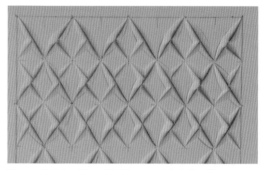

Figure 9-6. In this grid, I have added flip-flops to every diamond. I think it's a bit too much carving.

Figure 9-7. Notice how Jim Lindgren, the carver of this piece, added crescents along the outer edge—a great way to give a straight edge interest.

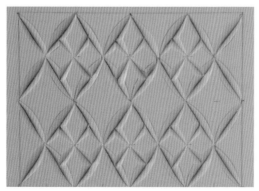

Figure 9-5. Flip-flops have been added to every other row.

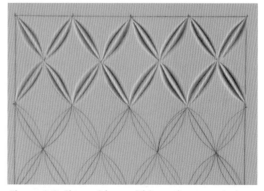

Figure 9-8. Sharp ridges within each crescent give the design a delicate appearance.

Figure 9-9. This interlocking circle grid is a little more challenging than the diamond grid.

Personally, I think it is too much carving. I believe that the amount of wood you leave uncarved is as important as the amount you carve. **Figure 9-7** is the top of a playing card box carved by Jim Lindgren of Alberta. Notice the way Jim added the crescents along the outer edge. It is a nice way to make a straight edge much more interesting. **Figure 9-8** is yet another way to carve the same pattern. The sharp ridges within each crescent give it a delicate appearance. I would choose to leave the center of each diamond just as it is. Adding any embellishments might distract from the pattern.

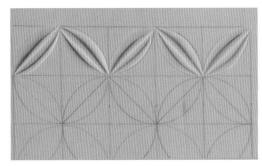

Figure 9-10. Sharp ridges are left in the petals to give the design a different look.

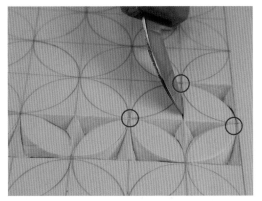

Figure 9-11. Removing a three-sided chip from inside the circle.

This interlocking circle grid is more challenging to carve, and it really isn't as difficult to draw as it first appears (See **Figure 9-9**.). To draw it on your practice board, begin with nine horizontal lines drawn 16mm apart. Then draw six vertical lines 16mm apart. You may use your bow compass to draw in the circles if you wish, but I chose to use a plastic circle template (see Figure 2-12 in Chapter Two: The Tools) and found that a 1¼"-diameter circle works perfectly.

There are a number of ways to carve this pattern. **Figure 9-10** shows the petals being carved with a ridge left in the center of each. This method is similar to the one shown in Figure 9-8, except that the shape of the uncarved center diamond is different. **Figure 9-11** illustrates another approach. I like this one so much that I started carving before I realized I should offer a couple of tips for the order of the cuts.

To remove the three-sided, curved triangle, begin with the cut going along the grain. Remember to keep your knife at a 65-degree angle, except when it's necessary to roll it up to 90 degrees in tight spots. I have indicated such tight spots with circles.

In **Figure 9-12**, notice that I come back diagonally across the grain for the second cut while making sure that I roll the knife up to nearly 90 degrees when starting and finishing. My third cut is then across the grain and leaves a sharp ridge across the center.

Chip Tip

When you have a three-sided chip that is long enough to be cut using only position one, make the cut that is with the grain first. If you were to make the other two cuts first and leave the with-the-grain cut until last, you will find that the wood will split along the grain as soon as you plunge your knife into it. If your cut splits rather than being cut, it will not be as clean, nor will it have the correct angle.

Chip Tip

If you find that the sharp ridges across the grain are breaking or chipping, it could be for a few reasons: 1) your knife needs stropping or honing, 2) the wood is too dry (See Chapter One: Choosing the Wood.), or 3) too much pressure is being applied.

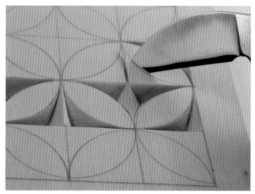

Figure 9-12. When you're making the inner cuts, I recommend that you make a smaller relief chip in the center of each triangle first and then make the larger chip.

Figure 9-13. I've turned the board 180 degrees to continue making my cuts.

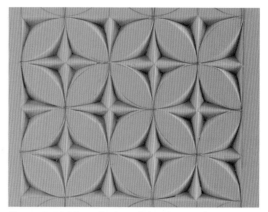

Figure 9-14. Though the section is complete, there's plenty of room for embellishments.

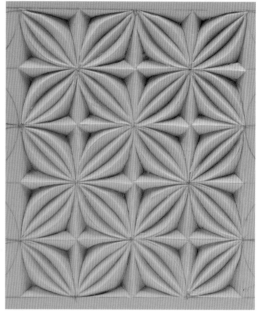

Figure 9-15. A sharp ridge was added to the center of each petal for a more delicate look to the carving in Figure 9-14.

Note that the board is turned 180 degrees in **Figure 9-13**, so you are now looking at the same pattern from the opposite direction. The first cut for the next chip is, once again, the cut that is made with the grain.

Figure 9-14 shows a completed carving section. While it is attractive enough on its own, there is plenty of room within those large petals to add embellishments or "ooohhs." There are a few choices that you can incorporate, so try a few and decide which you prefer. **Figure 9-15** shows the petals carved with a sharp ridge down the center. This treatment is nice but very delicate, so consider the project and how much handling it will get before you decide upon the completed design.

Grids can be used as background, too. Check out this African mask motif with woven grid.

For creating the grids in this chapter, use these diamond and circle grid line patterns to help you get started.

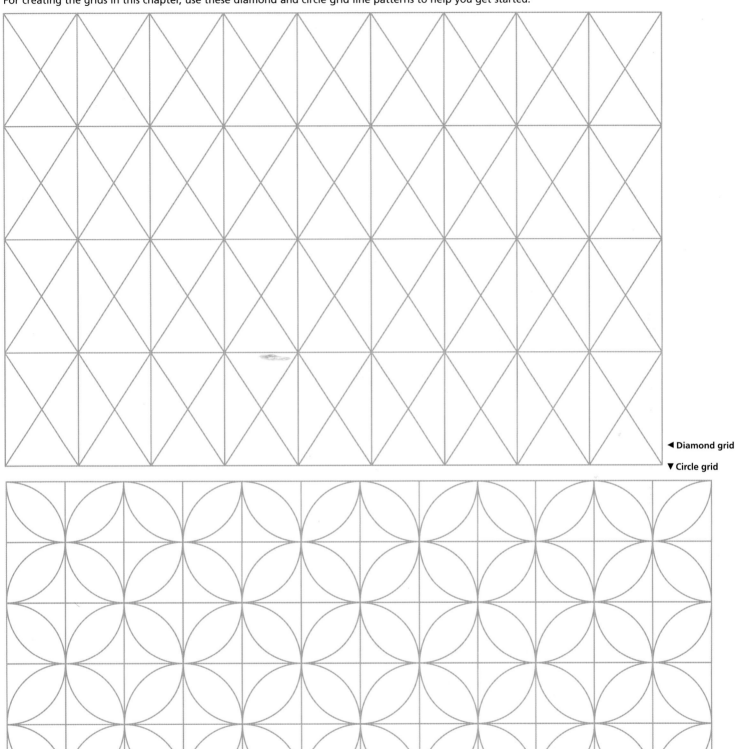

◀ Diamond grid

▼ Circle grid

10
ROSETTES

Traditional chip carving has its roots firmly established in ancient symbols and motifs. Many of the patterns can be traced to mythic or religious art forms. Rosettes form a large part of these motifs.

HOW TO DIVIDE CIRCLES

I am offering instruction on the following pages as to how you can divide circles into various numbers of equal parts. This is the groundwork that you can use to explore the very satisfying and enjoyable pastime of creating your own patterns. Do not be too surprised when you discover that you will be able to create dozens of different designs just by experimenting with your ruler, compass, and protractor.

One of the gratifications I get from chip carving is an avenue for creative expression. It's likely that you will be very pleased to find a talent within you that has perhaps gone unnoticed. I get a kick out of students who proclaim, "I'm not very artistic" or "I could never draw." It really is quite easy to learn, with just a few pointers and the desire to begin.

You will also discover that the same motif can be carved in a number of different ways. As with the diamond borders, you can switch between positive and negative designs that will change the pattern completely. Some change so dramatically that it is hard to believe they are carved from the same pattern.

Dividing a Circle into Three Equal Parts

1. Draw a vertical line.
2. Place your compass at point 1 and draw a circle (See **Figure 10-1.**).
3. Place the compass at point 2 and mark points B and C.
4. Draw lines from the center point outward to points A, B, and C to make three equal parts.
5. Draw lines from A to B, B to C, and C to A to make an equilateral triangle.

Or, using a protractor, mark the circle every 120 degrees.

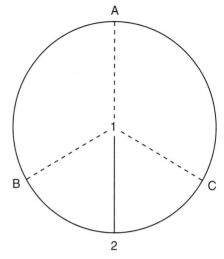

Figure 10-1.

Dividing a Circle into Four Equal Parts

1. Draw a vertical line.
2. Place your compass at point 1 and draw a circle (See **Figure 10-2.**).
3. To find points A and B, open the compass wider than the original radius (you do not need to increase it to any particular size, just make it wider). Place the compass at points 2 and 3 and make small arcs (X) outside the circle as shown.
4. Draw a line from point A to point B to form four equal parts.

Or, using a protractor, mark the circle every 90 degrees.

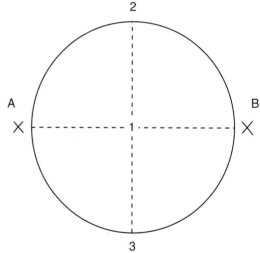

Figure 10-2.

Dividing a Circle into Five Equal Parts

1. Draw a vertical line.
2. Place your compass at point 1 and draw a circle (See **Figure 10-3.**).
3. To find points A and B, open the compass wider than the original radius (you do not need to increase it to any particular size, just make it wider). Place the compass at points 2 and 3 and make small arcs outside the circle as shown.
4. Align your ruler between points A and B and mark point C.
5. Return the compass to the original radius and place it at point 2. Then, mark points D and E.
6. Align your ruler between points D and E and mark point F.
7. Reset the compass radius so that it matches the distance between point F and point C. Then, make an arc to form point G.

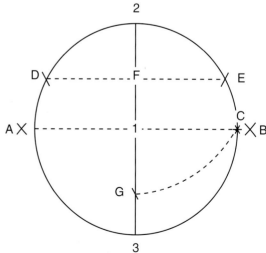

Figure 10-3.

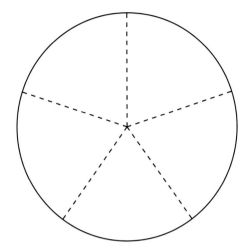

Figure 10-4.

8. Reset the compass once again to match the distance from point C to point G. The final radius you just established will give you five equal parts as shown in **Figure 10-4.**

Or, using a protractor, mark the circle every 72 degrees.

Dividing a Circle into Six Equal Parts

1. Draw a vertical line.
2. Place your compass at point 1 and draw a circle (See **Figure 10-5.**).
3. Do not change the compass radius; simply place it at point 2 and mark points 3 and 7, or even draw an arc from 3 to 7.
4. Place your compass at point 3 and mark point 4, or draw an arc from 4 to 2.
5. Continue placing the compass at each new point you create until you have completed the six-point rosette.

Or, using a protractor, mark the circle every 60 degrees.

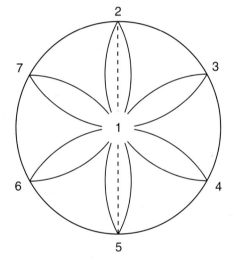

Figure 10-5.

Dividing a Circle into Seven Equal Parts

1. Draw a vertical line.
2. Place your compass at point 1 and draw a circle (See **Figure 10-6.**).
3. Do not change the compass radius; simply place it at point 2 and make small arcs at points A and B.
4. Align your ruler between points A and B and make a mark at point C.
5. Place your compass at point C and reset the opening to the distance between points C and B. This new opening will divide the circle into seven equal parts. We will make a seven-point rosette on the Letter Holder on page 90.

Or, using a protractor, mark the circle every 51.5 degrees.

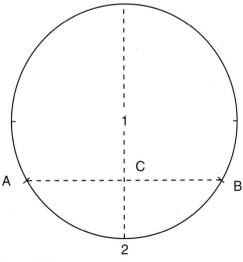

Figure 10-6.

Dividing a Circle into Eight Equal Parts

1. Draw a vertical line.
2. Place your compass at point 1 and draw a circle (See **Figure 10-7**.).
3. Establish points A and B by opening the compass wider than the original radius and placing it at points 2 and 3. Make small arcs (X) outside the circle—just like the four-part circle.
4. Align your ruler between A and B and mark points 4 and 5 on the edge of the circle.
5. Establish points C, D, E, and F by reducing the compass opening arbitrarily and placing it at points 2, 3, 4, and 5, making small arcs outside the circle.
6. Draw lines from C to F, D to E, and A to B to divide the circle into eight parts.

Or, using a protractor, mark the circle every 45 degrees.

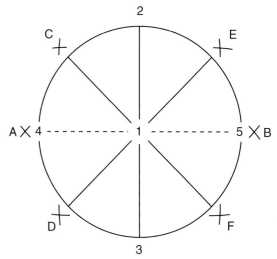

Figure 10-7.

Dividing a Circle into 12 Equal Parts

1. Begin by drawing a six-point circle using a horizontal line from point 2 to point 5 (See **Figure 10-8**.).
2. Establish points A and B by opening the compass wider than the original radius. Place the compass at points 2 and 5 and make small arcs (X) outside the circle as shown.
3. Return your compass to the original radius and begin to draw in the next six parts, starting at point A.

Or, using a protractor, mark the circle every 45 degrees.

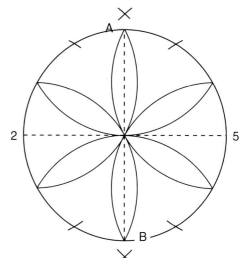

Figure 10-8.

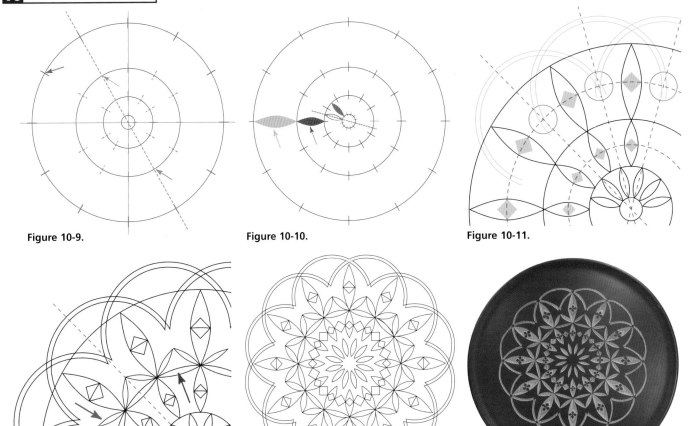

Figure 10-9.

Figure 10-10.

Figure 10-11.

Figure 10-12.

Figure 10-13. The final illustration. The full-size diameter of this rosette is approximately 7½".

Figure 10-14. Here is the rosette carved on a surface that had been painted first. We call this technique "reverse finishing," and we'll discuss it in Chapter Fourteen: Finishing.

DRAW A 12-POINT ROSETTE

Now that you have the know-how to divide a circle into various numbers of equal parts, let's draw an actual 12-point rosette. I have an original rosette pictured in **Figure 10-13** above. (At least I believe it is an original. Because rosettes have been around for centuries, it is sometimes impossible to determine if a pattern is original or not.) This particular pattern looks great either stained or left clear. In fact, I have carved it using a "reverse finishing" style, which is pictured in **Figure 10-14.**

Practice drawing this rosette on paper before you try it on wood. You will need a good quality 6" bow compass with B or B2 lead, a circle template with various sizes, and a large circle template.

As you look at the steps and see all of the colored arrows and lines, don't get excited. Go through the steps one at a time—it isn't nearly as difficult as it first appears.

First, establish a center point by drawing a horizontal line, and then draw a vertical line at exactly 90 degrees to the horizontal line using the arc method described in "Dividing a Circle into Four Equal Parts" (See page 57). I have indicated these with red lines (See **Figure 10-9.**).

Next, place your compass point at the center and draw four circles using the following approximate measurements: the first circle has a radius of 7mm; the next, 22mm; the third, 45mm; and the fourth, 80mm.

Divide the outer (fourth) circle into 12 equal parts using the instructions on page 59. Simply make 12 small arcs as indicated in blue.

Using your ruler, align the center point with the 12 arcs just drawn and mark the 12 divisions on both the third and second circles as indicated by the green dotted lines.

Draw in the petals between the fourth and third circles as indicated by the yellow arrow (See **Figure 10-10.**). To draw these petals, I used a 2¾" circle template aligned with the 12 arcs created in Figure 10-9.

Draw the petals between the third and second circles as indicated by the red arrow. To draw these petals, I used a 1½" circle template.

Your first, or smallest, circle should not have any of the arcs dividing it into 12 segments just yet. Remember in Figure 10-9 that we only established the arcs in the second, third, and fourth circles. Now, you can determine and draw them in the first circle. Notice, however, that they do not line up with the others; instead they are centered in between the other marks. You may either determine their location mathematically, as in the first group, or, like me, you can take an educated guess where the centers would be. Draw them by using your trusty washer/template. The light brown dotted line indicates one of those 12 divisions. Continue to draw in all 36 of the petals.

Now, establish the center of one petal in the second row by measuring with your ruler (See **Figure 10-11**.). Place your compass in the center point and draw a very faint circle as indicated by the blue dotted line. Do the same with the first row of petals.

Draw the diamond shapes in the center of each petal. To make sure that they are consistent in size, I would measure one and then use the compass to make small arcs (dots, actually) in the center of each petal.

Establish the marks indicated by the green circles by aligning your ruler through the center of the innermost petals as indicated by the dotted red lines. Next, draw the outer arcs indicated in yellow by placing the compass point in the center of the green circle. Notice that there are two arcs. The ones I have drawn have radii of 30mm and

32mm (giving a 2mm-wide chip).

You are almost finished. Draw in the petals indicated by the red arrows (See **Figure 10-12**.). Use a circle template and choose the most appropriate size for your personal rosette.

Finally, draw the petals indicated by the blue arrows. You should be able to use your washer/template for these. These last petals will be slightly smaller than the ones just drawn, indicated by the red arrows. When you are finished, your rosette should look like the one in Figure 10-13.

Now that you have drawn your rosette, remember that interlocking circle rosettes can provide different carving options. Often, they can be easily carved in the positive or the negative (See **Figure 10-15** and **Figure 10-16**.).

Figure 10-15 and Figure 10-16. A rosette of interlocking circles can be found in art forms and architecture throughout the world for hundreds of years. It is easy to draw and carve in either the positive or negative and adapts itself to many projects. For instructions on how to draw and carve this popular rosette, see the Plant Box project on page 86.

I've included a shaded drawing of the
rosette to help you visualize the chips
that you will carve out.

11

LAYOUT AND DESIGN

I enjoy laying out my pattern and getting ready to carve. Many chip carvers do not. I have to wonder if their dislike of the task has to do with needing some good ideas as to how to go about it. There has not been anything on the market, to my knowledge, that helps those carvers who could use some guidance with regard to the layout process. I hope the information in this chapter can help, but keep in mind that the process is rather subjective. I am happy to share my approach, but you should certainly consider any ideas that may be available. No one has a monopoly on knowledge.

LAYING OUT BORDERS

Let's first consider how to go about laying out a border on a square or rectangular project. One method is to draw the center lines both horizontally and vertically; then, beginning at the center, draw 4mm squares outward until you reach the desired length. The problem with this method is that the borders on the sides may not be exactly the same distance from the edge of the project as the borders across the top and bottom.

I prefer to draw the outside border line all the way around the project using the same measurement from the edge of the project. In projects that are about the size of a normal jewelry box, I would suggest a distance of 1cm from the outside edges.

From this outside border, you can then draw the remaining reference lines for your chosen border. Remember to allow for the 2mm-wide straight-line chips should your pattern include this type of chip. Take a look at **Figure 11-1** and **Figure 11-2**, which illustrate this method.

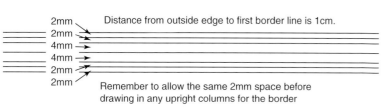

Distance from outside edge to first border line is 1cm.

2mm
2mm
4mm
4mm
2mm
2mm

Remember to allow the same 2mm space before drawing in any upright columns for the border

Figure 11-1. The placement of horizontal lines for laying out a border.

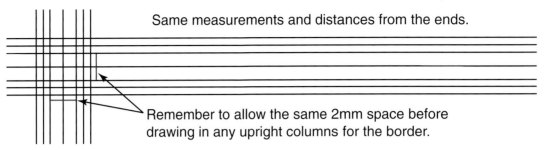

Same measurements and distances from the ends.

Remember to allow the same 2mm space before drawing in any upright columns for the border.

Figure 11-2. The placement of vertical lines for laying out a border.

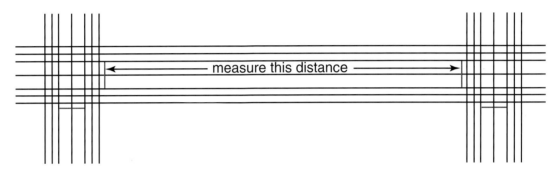

measure this distance

Figure 11-3. Measuring for pattern placement.

Once you have drawn in these lines, you can then fill in the pattern reference lines. Let's decide that we are going to carve the standard-sized positive diamond border as described in Chapter Six: Standard-Sized Borders. This will require 4mm squares running the length of the border. Each diamond requires four 4mm squares, thereby making the dimensions 8mm x 8mm. We want all of the diamonds to be same size, and we want complete diamonds across the entire length. We do not want to end up with only a portion of a diamond.

The next step would then be to measure the distance we have to work with (See **Figure 11-3.**). It would be so easy if every project that you did had a measurement that was exactly divisible by eight. We should be so lucky. However, figuring out the exact measurements we will use isn't too difficult because we will do it all in metric. Metric measurements are based on tenths, making division and multiplication quite simple.

Let's say hypothetically that the measurement in Figure 11-3 is 202mm (which is the same as 20.2cm because there are 10mm in each cm). Our diamond border needs 8mm for each complete diamond. Divide 202mm by 8mm, and we get 25.25 diamonds. So, if we were to carve 25 diamonds, each measuring 8mm, we would need 25 x 8 = 200mm.

Figure 11-4. The Ing border motif.

Because our measurement was 202mm, and we need only 200mm, we have 2mm left over. The easy solution is to leave an additional 1mm of space at each end. 1mm is next to nothing and would not be noticeable whatsoever.

But it won't always be that easy. What would we do if the measurement were not so close? Suppose it was 206mm. That means we would have 25 x 8 = 200mm with 6mm left over. While we could leave an additional space of 3mm (6mm divided in half) at each end, that amount of space is too much. The original space of 2mm plus another 3mm equals a 5mm space at each end.

If this happened to me, I would add another diamond for a total of 26 diamonds. Then, I would need a distance of 26 x 8 = 208mm. There are three ways we could handle this situation:

1. We could decrease the space left at each end from 2mm to 1mm, which would give us the 208mm needed for 26 full diamonds.

2. We could carve 25 diamonds, each 8mm wide, and one diamond that's 6mm wide. (I don't care for this solution because the narrow diamond would stick out too much.)

3. We could carve 24 diamonds, each 8mm wide (24 x 8 = 192mm), and carve two diamonds, each 7mm wide (2 x 7 = 14mm), for a total of 192 + 14 = 206mm.

The third option would be my choice. If you choose this option, it's a good idea to separate the two 7mm diamonds by carving a few 8mm diamonds between them. I guarantee they will never be noticed.

Solving that problem was reasonably easy, but what if we had wanted to use the Ing design? To refresh your memory, I am showing you the Ing again (See **Figure 11-4.**). Each individual design is 8mm high and 3cm long. Therefore, the measurements (2mm, 2mm, 4mm, 4mm, 2mm, 2mm) we did in the border layout in Figure 11-1 will work just fine for the height. What about those two hypothetical length measurements of 202mm and 206mm?

This problem isn't too difficult with a basic knowledge of arithmetic. Each individual Ing is 3cm, or 30mm, meaning that seven of them would require 7 x 30 = 210mm. We have only 202mm. Divide 202 by 210, and we find that 202 represents 96.2%. If we took the standard 30mm required for each Ing and reduced it to 96.2% (30 x 96.2% = 2.89mm), we would need seven Ing designs measuring 2.89mm to fit in that 202mm space nicely.

Now, I don't know how good your eyesight and hand steadiness are, but there's no way that I could measure 2.89mm. I can, however, measure 2.9mm. If I made seven Ings at 2.9mm that would equal 7 x 2.9 = 203mm. All I would have to do is make a 1mm adjustment somewhere along the row of them or make two adjustments of 0.5mm each.

As you can see, it really is not that difficult to figure out exactly how to fit a border within a specified space. As long as you keep each segment of the border close in size and do not make one segment significantly different, viewers will never notice the difference in sizes.

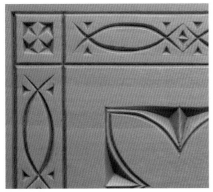

Figure 11-5. This Ing border has a positive diamond in the corner.

Figure 11-6. This negative diamond border has a positive diamond in the corner.

Figure 11-7. On this rope border, the rope just continues on. Note the stab mark for added interest.

Figure 11-8. The lace border simply continues to the very end, across the length of the top. The side borders start and end in a similar manner.

Figure 11-9. This straight-line border has a few bends to make it interesting.

Figure 11-10. This wider-than-average border that was carved in Chapter Seven: Large-Width Borders continues right around the corner.

HOW TO HANDLE THE BORDER CORNERS

There are many different ways to carve the corners of borders. Take a look at **Figure 11-5** to **Figure 11-10** for some examples. As you can see, there are many alternatives for designing the corners of your borders. The only thing I would caution you about is combining too many borders and/or corners on one project (See **Figure 11-11**.).

Another point certainly worth mentioning in regards to border layout and design is the necessity to run the borders down the back, front, and sides of your project if those areas are being carved. Furthermore, all of the borders should align with each other as illustrated in **Figure 11-12**.

In preparing the pattern or design for your project, you will, of course, have considered the main theme as one of the first steps. The first step, that is, after you have gone through the initial process below, which I also discuss in Chapter Fourteen: Finishing.

1. You have the actual project and recipient.
2. You know how the project will be finished.
3. Now we can think about and design the pattern.

Let's assume you have established the main theme, deciding upon a rosette in the center of the project and a border around the outside. Your pattern would look something like **Figure 11-13**.

So far, so good, but take a good look and see if you agree that something is needed in the four corners. I am sure you will agree that something is needed. Why? To fill in the space? Nope, not completely, even though the area is begging for something. The reason is to "please our eyes." We have a project with square corners and a border

Figure 11-11. Too many borders or corners can severely detract from your carving. This project has a chevron border (outer top), an egg–and–dart border (outer side), a positive diamond border (inner side and top), and a negative cross and St Andrew's cross (corner). A combination of any two would have been a better choice. It's unfortunate because the carving itself is quite good.

Figure 11-12. Don't forget to carve the borders on the back, front, and sides of your project and to make sure that they are in the proper alignment. Attention to these details will add polish to your finished work.

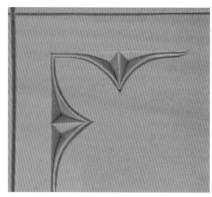

Figure 11-15. The center ridge is added to reduce the size of the main chip as well as create an additional shadow. The sharp ridge along the outside makes a big difference.

Figure 11-16. This design uses the same concept as Figure 11-15, but it has a different configuration. Check out the double straight-line border—it's a good way to reduce the size of the area as well as frame the work.

Figure 11-17. The corner on this box was carved using a foliage design made popular by Wayne Barton.

Figure 11-18. This corner pattern is another variation of the corners in Figure 11-15 and Figure 11-16.

with square corners. When we add a round rosette to the center, we need some sort of transition to "soften the blow" between the round and square design elements.

The four corners in **Figure 11-14** turn the outside right angles into a cove shape. The combination of all four coves takes our eyes from a square to an ellipse, or oval, to the rosette. This addition makes the piece much more pleasant to look at, while filling in those spaces at the same time. There are several ways that we can design and carve these transitional corners. **Figure 11-15** to **Figure 11-18** show just a few examples.

Figure 11-13. The layout of the main rosette and the border.

Figure 11-14. Transitional coves are added to soften the difference in shape between the square border and the round rosette.

Figure 11-19. The top of a silverware chest carved in basswood with a satin urethane finish.

Figure 11-21. To make the chest appear a little less heavy, I added brass feet in the corners. Raising a large piece, like this one, off of the surface makes it look lighter and easier to handle.

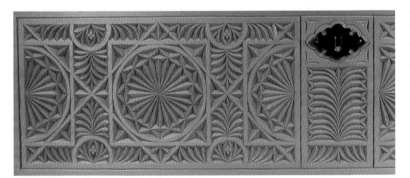

Figure 11-20. Here is the bottom portion of the front of the silverware chest. Notice how the many sharp ridges are broken up with ribbing. Ribbing adds interest and keeps the viewer from going cross-eyed.

CARVING LARGE AREAS

Designing a pattern for a large area can certainly be a challenge. The type of wood you are using will make a big difference. You may recall that I talked about the virtues of basswood and butternut in Chapter One: Choosing the Wood. Basswood, with its nondescript grain, is perfect for intricate designs and will show your carving well. Butternut, with its beautiful grain configuration, carves nicely but needs a pattern that will not fight with the grain for attention. Keep it plain and simple by avoiding sharp ridges.

Figures 11-19, 11-20, and **11-21** show a silverware chest measuring 14½" wide x 22" long x 7½" high. When my wife first saw the chest, she thought she was getting a huge jewelry box. Can you imagine how much jewelry it would take to fill a box this size, not to mention how much it would cost?

Getting back to the chest—as you can see, the top area was so large that I decided to break it up into five segments, each within its own frame. I wanted the challenge of lots of sharp ridges, but it had to have some ribbing, or wider ridges, to make it easier to look at, too. It also needed a variety of shapes as well as sizes. Too many chips of the same shape and size carved over and over can make you dizzy while looking at it. At the same time, it is important to keep a constant theme. To accomplish all of these guidelines, I have only three separate patterns, even though there are five segments. The two outside segments are portions of the large center pattern. The two segments on either side of the center are also the same.

To frame-in the entire box and bring the pattern together, I chose a banding often found in musical instruments. The banding comes in three-foot strips and is laminated ebonized maple, tulipwood, and maple. Because this piece is one-of-a-kind, I unfortunately do not have a pattern for it. However, please feel free to duplicate it or any part of it that you wish.

GETTING THE PATTERN ONTO THE WOOD 12

DRAWING DIRECTLY ON WOOD

I highly recommend this method for geometric patterns. Draw the pattern directly on the wood with good quality tools including a 0.5mm mechanical pencil with B lead refills, a 6" bow compass, a T-square with both metric and English or Imperial measurements, and a 6" ruler.

You cannot trace geometric shapes or straight lines with precision, and, because your carving of rosettes and geometric shapes should be as precise as possible, take your time to draw the patterns accurately. Free-form or free-style patterns are a different matter. Because there is generally some leeway with these, tracing the pattern onto your wood is quite acceptable.

TRACING THE PATTERN

Tracing free-form patterns should be done using graphite paper and not carbon paper. Carbon

paper is messy and smudges terribly, so avoid it completely. Graphite paper is available at all art supply stores as well as most craft stores.

I find it is a good idea to first trace the pattern onto parchment paper, also called tracing paper or onionskin paper. Having your pattern on transparent tracing paper allows you to view the exact placement on your wood and therefore line up the pattern with the borders and other design elements. When you have the exact placement, use a few strips of masking tape to hold the tracing paper in place. Then, insert the graphite paper between the tracing paper and the wood and proceed to trace the pattern. It is also a good idea to check to make sure you have the graphite paper with the right side up. Trust me on this.

If the wood is dark in color or if you are transferring the pattern onto a painted surface, then perhaps Saral is a better choice than graphite paper. Saral, which is a brand name, is a transfer paper often used on fabric. It comes in white, red, and blue and can be found at fabric and sewing centers as well as some craft stores.

HEAT TRANSFER KIT

In the year 2000, an inventor in the U.S. developed a heat transfer method for transferring patterns. The method uses a heat transfer tool similar to a woodburning pen, except that it has a large circular burning surface, and a transfer paper that was developed specifically for this purpose.

The method is simple: print the pattern onto a sheet of this special transfer paper and use the heat tool to transfer the pattern onto your wood. There is some wood preparation necessary first, but it isn't rocket science and can be done by anyone. The instructions are included with the transfer kit. While the system is easy to use, it only makes sense for the carver who will use it regularly. If you plan to transfer only a small number of patterns, it probably makes more sense to use the tracing method described earlier. If you have a number of patterns to do, or absolutely despise the drawing part of the process, then the system is worth the investment. I use this system.

For the ideal setup you should have the following: a computer; a scanner; basic knowledge of a graphics program, such as Corel Draw or Photoshop (you do not have to be a computer guru, but you should have basic knowledge); and a laser printer (ink jet printers will not work).

The first task is to select your pattern and scan it into your computer. Use a graphics program to enlarge, reduce, stretch, or alter the pattern in any way you wish. Also use the graphics program to remove any pattern lines that will not be carved off. Once the pattern has been transferred onto your wood, the only way to remove lines that are not carved off is to sand them off, and even that method is tough. So, make sure to remove the lines you won't carve and to carve off the lines in the pattern.

Once you have adjusted the pattern to the final version, print it out on your laser printer using the special paper that comes with the kit. Again, ink jet printers will not work. Then, position the pattern onto your wood and use the heat tool to do the transfer. The transfer will be an exact copy of the pattern, and you will be surprised how clear and crisp the lines are. You can see this heat transfer system on the Chipping Away website (See the Sources of Supply section on page 106.). **Figure 12-1** shows how clear the pattern transfer will be using the heat transfer kit.

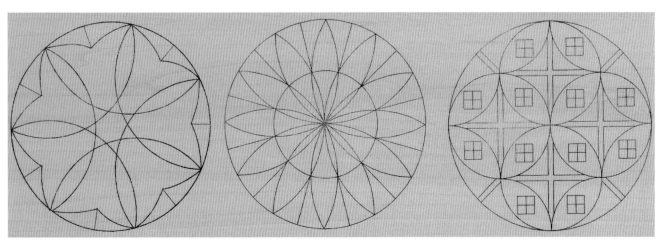

Figure 12-1. Three patterns transferred using the heat transfer kit.

OTHER METHODS FOR TRANSFERRING THE PATTERN

Most chip carvers will tell you that it often takes longer to put the pattern on the wood than it does to do the carving. There are several methods for transferring the pattern quicker than tracing by hand. Try them yourself to see if you have a preference, but here is my view on them:

Gluing the Pattern On

Bad idea. This method is fine for scroll saw work, but it isn't very good for chip carving. With the paper glued onto the wood, you cannot see the grain, nor can you see how precise your chips are. I suppose that it may be more acceptable with free-form motifs than geometric patterns, but I personally do not care for it in either case.

Ironing the Pattern On

Not reliable. This procedure requires first photocopying the pattern, which must be done on a copier using a toner and not carbon paper. Many fax machines have the ability to make copies on plain paper and do so using a carbon paper refill. These photocopies will not work with an iron. The photocopier must use a powdered toner, and the copy must be fairly recent so that the toner will transfer to the wood. A copy that was made some time ago will not work very well at all.

Heat a standard iron to the cotton level and, with the photocopy facedown, iron the paper to transfer the toner to the wood. Because the heat is generally uneven over the iron's surface, many times parts of the pattern will transfer while other parts will not. Then, if you attempt to go back over the area to correct, the toner that was transferred lifts off.

Using Lacquer Thinner

Not the greatest. The procedure here is to lay the photocopied pattern facedown on the wood and then rub a rag that has been dampened with lacquer thinner over the paper. The lacquer thinner soaks down through the paper and releases the toner onto the wood.

An alternative is to dampen the wood first, lay the photocopied pattern facedown, and then rub the paper with a dry cloth. It must be lacquer thinner and not mineral spirits, turpentine, or other such products because lacquer thinner is the only one that works.

The main problems encountered are 1) too much lacquer thinner results in the toner literally melting and bleeding into the wood like paint, 2) not enough lacquer thinner makes the toner transfer unevenly, 3) it is very messy, 4) it is very toxic and must be done in a well-ventilated area or outdoors, and 5) it's extremely difficult to clean up, even with sanding.

Self-Adhesive Transparencies

This method works well for patterns that do not have a lot of sharp ridges. Your local drafting or architect supply outlet will have these self-adhesive transparencies. They come under brand names, such as Chartpak and Repro Film. The transparency is a Mylar film, similar to those used for overhead projectors.

Simply make a photocopy of the pattern you have chosen onto the blank self-adhesive transparency you purchased. Make sure, of course, that the pattern is of the correct size and is copied to the correct side. Peel the backing off the transparent film and stick the pattern to the wood. Because it is transparent, you will be able to see the wood, its grain, and any blemishes you may have to use caution around. Now you are ready to carve right through this transparency. A nice side benefit is that is no cleanup is required after your carving is finished—simply peel off the transparency. You may experience some of the adhesive gumming up your knife, so be sure to wipe your blade periodically. Getting adhesive on the blade, however, is not a serious problem at all.

Chip Tip

Preparing the wood properly before drawing the pattern on is very important, too. Please read the section on "Cleaning Up Your Work" in Chapter Fourteen: Finishing for suggestions about lead selection, proper sanding, etc.

Chip Tip

Your carving cannot be better than your drawing, in most cases, so take the time to draw accurate patterns.

13
LETTERING

Carving a name on a project takes it to the next level. Now Mary or Johnny or Susan has a prized possession that he or she will cherish forever. Whether it is a simple coaster or a fancy jewelry box, it's theirs—and it says so!

If you have begun at the beginning of this workbook, there isn't too much to tell you about how to carve lettering. Notice the words "too much." There are a couple of things I will point out that may help. For now, let's talk about choosing the lettering style and size, accurately spacing the letters and words, and laying the name or word out on your project.

CHOOSING THE STYLE

Choose a style that fits the pattern you are carving as well as the person you are carving it for. Roman lettering is ancient and was designed and used for

formal documents and announcements. The original style was made up entirely of what we now call uppercase, or capital, letters. There wasn't a lowercase. Today, of course, there is a lowercase for every font style. Roman lettering is formal in appearance, and, while it is suitable for many situations, it does not portray what I would term a "friendly," or "warm," feeling.

For example, if I were carving a company's name on a project, Roman lettering would be quite suitable. It would also be very appropriate for a family name on a chest. If, however, I were making a project for a small child and carving his or her first name on it, I would choose a style that's much less formal. Take a look at **Figure 13-1** to **Figure 13-4** for some examples of lettering styles.

PROPER CHOICE OF UPPER- AND LOWERCASE

The improper use of upper- and lowercase letters can be disastrous. In Roman style, using all uppercase is quite suitable, but is absolutely not suitable with the script in Figure 13-4. Old English lettering is another example where using all uppercase is not suitable. Both styles are actually difficult to read when only uppercase is used. The general rule is that if both upper- and lowercase are available in the chosen font, you should make use of them.

PROPER SPACING OF THE LETTERS

Proper spacing of letters makes a huge difference. A few years ago, when I was judging a carving competition, there was a beautiful jewelry box entered that won a third-place ribbon. The initials in **Figure 13-5** were carved across the front of the box.

After the judging was over, the carver asked me to critique his work and suggest how he could improve. I pointed out a couple of items and made a few suggestions, which he was thankful for. I also complimented him on some areas where he did very well and finished by saying that

K I M

Figure 13-5. Here, "K I M" looks like a set of initials rather than a name.

This spacing is normal.

This spacing is too close.

This spacing is too far.

Figure 13-6.

CHIPPING AWAY
Chipping Away

Figure 13-1. I suppose if Chipping Away were the name of a law firm, the top style (Roman) would be suitable. For a friendly carving retailer, I believe the second choice would be my favorite.

EMILEE
Emilee

Figure 13.2. For a young girl by the name of Emilee, I would choose the second style for its feminine look. Yet, if Emilee were older and the project were to have her last, or family, name carved on it, then the first style would be quite appropriate as well.

ZANE
Zane

Figure 13.3. For a young boy by the name of Zane, I would choose the second style. In my eyes, this style is quite boyish, and it isn't one that I would choose for young Emilee.

Figure 13-4. The first style is fine for a young female, but it is too feminine for a male.

whoever was going to receive the jewelry box was very lucky and would cherish it. He said that it was for his daughter "Kim." Whoops! I thought it was for someone with the initials "K. I. M."

As you can see from the story, spacing is critical. When we read, we read words, not letters. In fact, we often recognize and read phrases rather than the individual words within the phrases—for example, "for example" and "matter of fact." The same concept applies to words. You are reading words right now, not the letters that make them up. Notice also how close the letters are in this text. The general rule is that letters should be carved as close together as possible, but be sure to carve comfortably (See **Figure 13-6**.).

PROPER SPACING OF WORDS
The general rule for spacing between words is that the space should be half the height of the capital letter. For example, if you are carving words or names with capital letters that are 2" in height, the space between the two words should be 1".

If you are carving initials, they are considered as words. While we are talking about initials, remember to carve the period to show that they are initials. Chip carvers like periods that are triangular rather than round, and, while we are talking about that, chip carvers are also allowed great design freedom when carving tight, round, circular things. For instance, you will not see me carve a flower with round petals; they will always be pointed. The same with feathers and eyes. Chip carvers have been given the right to change tight, round, circular objects into pointed things.

Lowercase letters often present small, round challenges. For instance, look at the a, f, and j in **Figure 13-7**. Notice that they have little round balls on them. You will also find them on other letters. You have permission to change these challenges into points—no problem. Dot the i and the j with a triangle, not a circle.

Just in case you run into the situation, the space between sentences should be the full height of the capital letter, as should be the distance between lines of carved text.

Your computer is a fantastic source of fonts. It is also an excellent means to enlarge the font to the size you want, and it gives you the spacing automatically. I would be lost without mine. Once you have the font and the size, print it out on paper. I prefer to put the name or word on parchment paper, or tracing paper, in the actual manner that it will be transferred onto my project. Then, I draw center lines both horizontally and vertically on both the text and the project. Line up the reference lines with each other, use masking tape to hold the tracing paper on the project, and use graphite paper to make the transfer. See Chapter Twelve: Getting the Pattern onto the Wood for more information.

CARVING THE LETTERS
By now you should have a pretty good understanding of how to approach the actual carving. All of it is done while holding your knife in position one, unless, of course, it is convenient to use position two due to grain consideration. I would suggest that you look at each chip to be removed and break it down to its simplest form. Let's work through the carving of a letter.

This letter F (See **Figure 13-8**.) is in a Roman-style font. (I have included the layout for the entire alphabet in this style within this chapter, see pages 76 to 77). If you do not have a computer, you may trace the letters on parchment paper, and then transfer them to your project. Or, if you wish, you can use a graph-style layout and draw them directly. Remember, your carving will generally reflect your drawing, so take the time to draw your letters neatly. Drawing each and every serif is up to you, but it is probably a good idea while you are still learning.

Notice that I have not drawn the serifs (See **Figure 13-9**.). Again, it's up to you whether or not to draw in the serifs, but it is a good idea to draw them when you are first learning to carve this style. You will soon see, however, that we ignore the serifs until the entire letter is carved (See **Figure 13-10** to **Figure 13-19**.).

Serif

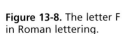

Serif

Figure 13-8. The letter F in Roman lettering.

Figure 13-7.

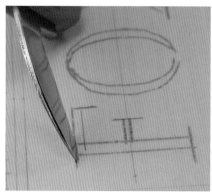

Figure 13-9. Carve the stop cuts on the largest chips first. On the F, that would be across the top first. Begin cutting at the extreme end where the serif will begin.

Figure 13-10. Ending at the extreme end where the letter will end. Notice that the knife blade is cutting at the standard 65-degree angle we discussed earlier.

Figure 13-11. The next step is to cut the stop cut across the bottom of the F. Begin at the extreme end where the serif will begin. End at the extreme end where the letter will end.

Figure 13-12. Carve out the column, beginning at the top stop cut.

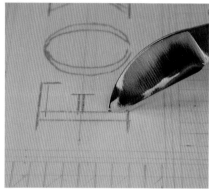

Figure 13-13. End at the bottom stop cut.

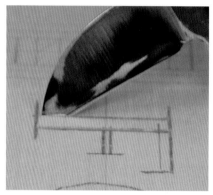

Figure 13-14. Turn the board and cut out the other side.

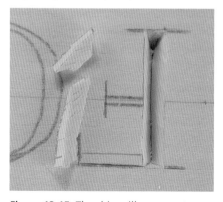

Figure 13-15. The chip will come out.

Figure 13-16. Do the same for the remaining chips. First make the stop cuts, and then the chip.

Figure 13-17. Always do the stop cut first.

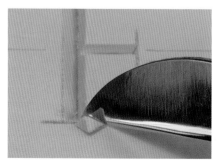

Figure 13-18. Now that the letter is carved, it's time to go back and chip out the serifs. Use both position one and position two, just like the flip-flops.

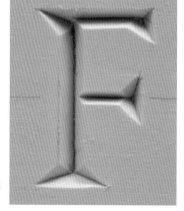

Figure 13-19. And the final result—not too shabby!

14
FINISHING

CLEANING UP YOUR WORK

Before you even think about applying a finish, you must first clean up your work and prepare the wood surface. One of the best aids in cleaning up is to have the project properly prepared before you begin your carving, and, in fact, even before you do the drawing.

I remember that back when I was first learning the art of chip carving, I had a dickens of a time even erasing the pencil lines that had not been carved off. If the surface of your wood has been sanded with anything less than 220-grit sandpaper, you will find that your pencil lines are actually drawn within the scratches left by the sandpaper. The result is that, when using an eraser, you're really not even reaching the lines. You will have a similar experience if you use anything harder than HB lead in your pencil, and HB isn't the greatest.

For those who may not be familiar with pencil lead, HB is the most common lead found in standard pencils. Draftsmen use harder leads to get finer lines that do not wear as rapidly. H is the first level harder than the standard HB. After H comes H2 and H4, indicating harder and still harder levels. On the other end of the spectrum, B is the next softest lead in the range from the HB standard. Following B is B2 and B4, indicating even softer levels.

I recommend a 0.5mm lead mechanical pencil because it will give you thin lines with B-level lead. B2 is even better than B, but it breaks too easily for me. For my compass, I use a B2 lead because the lead is much thicker than pencil lead. When sharpening your compass lead, don't bring it to a point like a pencil sharpener. Sharpen it to an angle, with the highest point being the closest to the compass point (See **Figure 14-1**.). You will

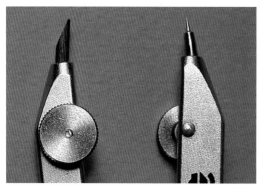

Figure 14-1. Notice that the lead in a compass is sharpened to one side.

get more consistently accurate lines with this method. Also notice the small collar on the compass point. This collar will help prevent the point from penetrating too far into the wood.

To prepare your wood, first of all, sand the wood surface using consistently finer grits until you reach a minimum of 320. Then, draw your pattern on the wood. When you are carving, it is great if you can cut the pencil lines off as you follow the pattern. You will have fewer lines to erase if you carve most of them off. There will, of course, be some reference lines that do not get carved off, and they can be removed with a white polymer eraser if you prepared the wood surface properly and drew light lines. Heavy lines and those lines drawn with too much force will present more of a challenge. Stubborn lines from graphite paper marks may come off easier with an ink eraser. I often use a cotton swab moistened with isopropyl alcohol to reach into tight and hard-to-get places.

It is best to avoid sanding your finished carving if it has sharp ridges in its pattern. Sharp ridges can quickly become flat ridges and lose their effect if they're sanded. Once you have your piece cleaned, use a soft brush or a tack rag to remove any sanding dust or dirt.

CLEAR FINISH OR STAIN?

This question should have been decided upon long ago. Actually, your choice of finish should be one of the first questions you ask yourself when choosing the pattern. Let me explain.

Prior to 1990, you would have been hard-pressed to find many chip-carved pieces that were stained. It didn't matter if the project was a decorative or a functional piece; it was given a clear finish. It didn't even matter whether the piece originated in Eastern Europe, Scandinavia, the UK, or North America; odds were that the piece was unstained. There were two main reasons that pieces were kept clear: the chip carving patterns of the time and the staining characteristics of basswood.

Chip Carving Patterns in Use

The perception of the day was that chip carving patterns with sharp ridges, and plenty of them, demonstrated the skill level of the carver. The more sharp ridges there were in the pattern, the better.

Once carved, a pattern with a multitude of sharp ridges had to have a clear finish for the piece to be appreciated. Staining such a carving would actually hide all of the individual shadows created by these sharp ridges. Let me explain further. We have all applied stain to a board, and, when doing so, we have a fair amount of control over how much stain we allow to be absorbed into the surface of the wood. We could allow the stain to soak in for a few minutes and then wipe off the excess stain; or we could choose to wipe the stain off almost immediately, thereby applying a very light coat. When we applied stain to the end grain of the board, however, that was a different story. The stain would soak in quickly, resulting in the ends of the board being much darker than the surface.

When we chip carve, we are creating end grain in every chip. Hence, when stain is applied, it soaks in with very little control from us. I did not

Chip Tip

I often hear from chip carvers that their wood seems to get dirty during the carving process. Perhaps the constant handling of the project is the cause or perhaps the lead smudges. If you encounter this problem, it may help if you use a mixture of 50% urethane and 50% mineral spirits to seal the surface after you sand, but before you draw. You may need another light, final sanding following the application, but this little trick will help in the cleanup process.

Chip Tip

Cleaning up your work also means going back over any chips that may not have come out cleanly. This may prove overwhelming at times, and it's actually best to clean up any cut that needs it as you are carving. I recall one student who was having a particularly tough time getting his cuts perfected. He had the "loose-toothed beaver" dilemma I spoke of in Chapter Five: Three Main Shapes of Chip Carving. This student returned a few days later and told me he found the culprit that was causing his problem!

Chip Tip

Remember that large cardboard box I suggested you use when increasing the moisture content of wood back in Chapter One: Choosing the Wood? The same box makes an excellent dust-proof spray paint booth. Simply place your piece inside the box, using the same suspending support you made, and, after you have sprayed it, close the box flaps.

say "without control" because we can alter this characteristic. I will explain how in the next section. Given these characteristics, you can imagine that most of the shadows on a carving with sharp ridges would appear more like ink blots than individual highlights when viewed from a distance. A pinwheel, or swirl, pattern would be a good example of a pattern with many sharp ridges (See **Figure 14-2**.).

Figure 14-2. It is easy to see how this pattern would become lost if it were stained rather than left clear.

Staining Problems

Another reason for the absence of stained pieces is the staining problems associated with basswood. Basswood is also found throughout the UK and Europe under different names (limewood, linden, lindenholz, to name a few), and the staining problem is not particular to North America. When basswood is stained, it presents a blotch, or blotches, each about the size of a silver dollar, in a spot, or spots, that cannot be determined by the carver until the blotches actually appear.

Blotches, obviously, are unattractive. The only thing we can be reasonably sure of with these blotches that inevitably appear is that they will appear on the top and near the center of your project. This blotching is, no doubt, one of the reasons that basswood lost its value in the woodworking industry. In the 1920s and 1930s, it was standard to use basswood in North America for trim in homes, window and door

casings, cupboards, and even pieces of furniture, such as dining room sets. Who wouldn't rather use basswood with its nice, tight, clear grain, its basically knot-free appearance, and its abundance? When basswood is given a shellac or a paint finish, there are no problems, but when it is stained—the results are terrible. Once stains were developed using a petroleum base and became very popular, basswood was given the old heave-ho in the woodworking field. However, basswood cannot be topped for carving, so we adjust.

So Why Stain Basswood?

You may have already decided by now that there really isn't a problem and that you will simply give your projects a clear finish. That's what I thought, too. Then, back in the early '90s, when I was in the process of accepting a well-paying commission for a jewelry box, the topic of the finish arose. The lady asked me what type of finish I would suggest and, upon hearing my clear finish suggestion, quickly objected. "My bedroom suite is in walnut; I don't want a jewelry box that looks like pine." Even when I explained that basswood is difficult to stain and that staining would hide some of the carving features, she was not to be swayed. "Perhaps I should find someone else that could make it," she quipped. Hmmm…she must have forgotten just how famous I was! Because the commission was a good one, I didn't want to lose it and asked for time to come up with a solution. The lady became the proud owner of one of my creations that was designed and stained with a walnut finish especially for her. And I got the large commission.

Staining can be beautiful. The darker color on the inside of the chips, or the end grain, can really make your work stand out. Simply avoid too many sharp ridges. Refer back to Chapter Eight: Curved Borders to see examples of variations of the scalloped border (See Figures 8-3, 8-4, and 8-6). The scallop with the sharp ridge would be excellent for a clear finish, but would end up getting lost if stained. The scallop with the wide ridge, however, would be very suitable for staining.

DECIDE ON THE FINISH AT THE BEGINNING

I mentioned earlier that the finish should be decided upon early in the planning stage. My planning process would go something like this:

1) Either I am asked to carve or wish to carve something for a particular person or I come into possession of something and immediately think of someone that could make use of it.

2) I ask myself, "Where is this piece going to be placed or used by the recipient?" The answer to this question will generally dictate the finish. For example, the lady with the walnut jewelry box dictated a walnut finish; a decorative plate to be hung on a wall would need a finish to contrast with or match that wall; something used in the kitchen would need a finish to keep it clean-looking. What if a painted surface would be the choice? In fact, how about painting the piece first and then carving it? "Reverse finishing" is what I call this type of finish. I will give examples in a minute.

3) Now I can think about the pattern. For example, a stained finish means keeping sharp ridges to a minimum; a clear finish means go ahead and use the sharp ridges if it means that the piece won't be too delicate for the use it will receive; and a painted finish means it will be a little more difficult to carve, and the chips must be executed perfectly because mistakes will stand out.

Clear Finish

Use an aerosol spray can to apply the clear finish. Do not use a brush. I realize that aerosol cans are more expensive than using a brush; however, brush applications leave little puddles of finish in the bottom of the chips, resulting in a less-than-perfect appearance. When applying the spray, use "light coats." I define a light coat as "when you don't think you have applied enough." Sure enough, if you give it another spray, you will end up with a drip, and the time it takes to correct is just not worth the risk.

Urethane is my choice for a clear finish—petroleum-based and not water-based. I prefer the petroleum-based spray because it has an immediate yellowing effect on the basswood. I like the yellow, older, softer, warmer appearance. Water-based urethane spray does not give me this yellowing but instead leaves the wood in its natural color.

The number of coats you apply will depend on the piece, its usage, and even where you live. Is it a decorative wall hanging that will not be handled often, or is it a jewelry box that will be opened several times a week? Is it a kitchen project that will be used with food, or is it a mailbox that will be hung outdoors? Do you live on the coast in a humid atmosphere or in the plains where humidity is very low? All of these factors must be considered in determining the number of coats that would be appropriate.

Stained Finish

Before you begin to stain, it is very important to seal the wood, especially basswood. There are many different brands and types of sealers on the market, and your choice will depend on the stain you will be using. I prefer gel stains made by either Bartley (available in the U.S. only) or Minwax (available across North America). Both of these stains have a urethane base, and I therefore use a couple light coats of urethane clear finish as the sealer, followed by a light sanding.

Gel stains are not meant to be stirred or shaken, and therefore you cannot mix two different colors together without losing the benefit of the gel. What you can do, however, is start with a coat of one color and then add a coat of the second. By experimenting on scrap pieces, you will be able to get exactly the finish you want. It's a good idea to write down the details on how you arrived at that finish for future reference because, sure as God made little green apples, you will forget.

Chip Tip

The finish can make a world of difference. A perfectly carved piece can appear much less perfect if poorly finished. A mediocre carved piece, however, can appear first-rate if it has a perfect finish. Take the time to finish your piece properly.

Do not use a clear finish that is high gloss—ever. Glossy finishes are distracting. You will find that viewers are more attracted by the shine than by your carving. Glossy finishes also magnify errors or blemishes. Use a satin, or matte, finish because it will still give you a nice luster without the glare.

Adding Color to Your Carved Project

Adding color can be very attractive if used appropriately. One method that I use to add color is pencil crayons. These instruments are not the type used by schoolchildren, however. There are brands of pencil crayons that are oil-based and therefore can be worked to give a nice, even coloring. First, finish your carving with a clear urethane as previously described; then add a touch of color to the chosen areas. I prefer to use the pencil crayon as is and color the wood. Then, I use a cotton swab dipped in turpentine to smudge the color into a nice, even finish. You may also dip the pencil crayon into turpentine first and then color the area. The hues you choose should be pastel shades, not dark ones (See **Figure 14-3**.). Give it a try; I think you will like the results.

Painting the wood first and then chip carving it has a dramatic effect (See **Figure 14-4** to **Figure 14-6**.). Use a flat, water-based, acrylic paint with no gloss in a color that matches the decor of the room where it will displayed. Use a white pencil to draw the pattern or, if you are tracing the pattern, use Saral instead of graphite paper. Saral is a transfer paper that comes in white, blue, red, and other colors. You can find it at craft stores and in most fabric and sewing centers.

Figure 14-4. Here is an example of reverse finishing, that is, painting the wood first and then chip carving.

Figure 14-5. Other tools come in handy for chip carving. Because these small crescent shapes were difficult to chip carve neatly, I used a carving gouge, with a #7 sweep to get the curve I wanted. Then, I cut the bottom edge with my cutting knife.

Figure 14-3. Here is an example of color being added using oil-based pencil crayons. Keep the colors light pastel shades. Dark colors or actual paint can look tacky.

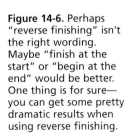

Figure 14-6. Perhaps "reverse finishing" isn't the right wording. Maybe "finish at the start" or "begin at the end" would be better. One thing is for sure— you can get some pretty dramatic results when using reverse finishing.

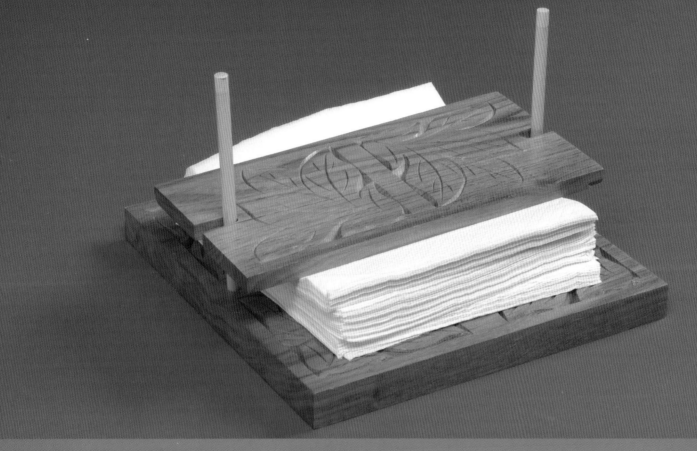

PROJECT 1: NAPKIN HOLDER

Here is a super project that you will use often and perhaps even wonder how you got along without it. As you can see from the photo, this is not a complicated project to make, and, while I have chosen butternut, you can certainly substitute basswood, pine, aspen, poplar, or even mahogany.

MATERIALS

Wood: Butternut
Base: 8" x 8" x ⅜"
Top: 3¾" x 8" x ⅜"
Two Posts: ¼" dowels, 4½" long

DESIGN INSPIRATION

Most, if not all, carvers enjoy the out-of-doors. After all, isn't that where the trees grow that produce such wonderful carving wood as basswood and butternut? As lovers of the outdoors, we are often campers or, at the very least, picnickers. One of life's little challenges for us outdoor types is finding a way to keep the napkins from blowing away as we prepare to enjoy a meal in the wild, or perhaps just in the city park. Fret no more, oh ye woodcarvers, as our napkin holder will not only keep those serviettes in place, but also show off your chip carving skills while doing so. The indoor types among us will find this useful project to be a focal point during meals being enjoyed without mosquito repellent.

2

The dowels should fit snugly in the base.

5

The layout for the top.

6

The layout for the base is complete. Drill holes for the ¼" dowels, leaving 8mm from the outside of the posts to the edge of the base.¾"

Step 1: Cut out the base and top to the dimensions shown in the Materials List.

Step 2: Drill the ¼" holes in the base for the posts. It is a good idea to check the fit of the dowels you are going to use by drilling a hole in a piece of scrap wood first. Commercial dowels do not always match the diameter stated.

Step 3: Notch the top to fit around the posts. Use a drill bit to start the notch, and then use a scroll saw or bandsaw to cut the hole. Each notch should be ⅜" wide and ¾" long.

Step 4: Sand the base and top with 120-grit, then 220-grit, and then 320-grit sandpaper to prepare the surface for your pattern. Remember to sand the edges as well as both the top and bottom.

Step 5: Draw the border around the perimeter of the base with a pencil and a ruler. You will note that I have drawn the border 8mm in from the edge of the base, which will line up my pattern with the outside of the posts. I have also drawn in the border along the sides of the top. Once again, I used the 8mm dimension for uniformity.

Step 6: Draw or trace the pattern onto the base. See Chapter Twelve: Getting the Pattern onto the Wood for helpful suggestions. Note: You will notice that I have drawn some of the wider areas to be carved. Because this pattern is free-form style, it is not necessary to draw every line. Free-form permits your own interpretation of the pattern to some extent and does not need to be as precise as geometric motifs. Okay, now that we've finished the pattern, let's get chipping away!

Finishing up: When the carving is completed, remove any pencil marks that have not been carved off. This should be quite easy because of the sanding preparation you did before drawing the pattern. One nice thing about this pattern is the lack of sharp ridges, meaning that you can perform a light sanding after carving without fear of causing damage.

Apply the finish of your choice. I have chosen Varathane's Professional Clear Finish (aerosol can) in Satin. I applied three light coats, then did a very light sanding with 320-grit followed by another three light coats of finish. Avoid glossy finishes on carved projects as discussed in Chapter Fourteen: Finishing.

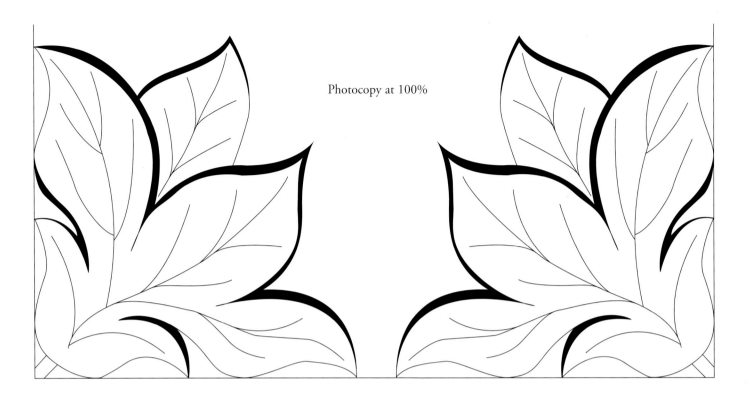

Photocopy at 100%

Chip Tip

Here are some things to keep in mind while creating this project:

- Hold your knife in position one for the entire project.
- Start with the largest chips along the outside edge. Make smaller chips within the larger areas, if necessary, to keep your final cuts clean.
- Remember to carve at an angle of 65 degrees, except when carving in tight areas where rolling your knife up to 90 degrees will prevent breakouts.
- When you are making the first cut in a new chip, your knife blade should face away from the previous cuts.

PROJECT 2: PLANT BOX

DESIGN INSPIRATION

Every once in a while, one of our students at Chipping Away is just a natural. They pick up the knife and start making cuts that took me months to learn. Actually my son, Todd, who helped build our business, is one such natural. Getting back to the story, a young fellow by the name of Bryan Hagan took a chip carving class back in the spring of 2003 and, within a very short period of time, was doing absolutely beautiful work. Bryan comes to visit us and to pick up supplies on a regular basis, and he often brings in his latest creation. On his last trip, he brought in the small plant box shown here.

Bryan Hagan's Planter

A closeup of Bryan's rosette, which he created in a CAD computer program.

This project is a very simple one (made from standard practice boards) that Bryan Hagan, one of our students, has offered to share with us. I have taken the liberty of making minor size and design changes. This little plant box will look great in any home or make a wonderful gift.

<table>
<tr><th colspan="2" style="background:black;color:white">MATERIALS</th></tr>
<tr><td colspan="2">

Wood: Basswood and Butternut

Front and Back: 1 Basswood Practice Board: 4" x 12" x ⅜"

Sides: 1 Butternut Practice Board: 4" x 12" x ⅜"

Bottom: Basswood Practice Board or any scrap wood

</td></tr>
</table>

Step 1: Cut out your plant box using the full-size patterns and dimensions shown here. Glue and clamp the pieces together with the butternut sides on the outside of the front and back panels as shown on the pattern. For the bottom, trace the planter outline and cut; don't worry about the bevels. Glue the bottom on the inside of the planter. The planter is used to hold potted plants or artificial plants, not earth and live plants, which is why neither the type of wood nor the bottom being a perfect fit matters.

Step 2: Choose your pattern. I am showing you two different patterns that you may choose from, or you may wish to use both patterns because they complement each other nicely. The plant box that I carved has the interlocking rosette pattern on the front and the floral patterns on the back and sides. You could do the same, or you could carve the rosette on the front and back and the flowers on the sides.

Step 3: Draw the straight-line border along all sides, following the actual shape of the panels. I have drawn a 2mm-wide border, starting 8mm in from the outside edge. Note: I have chosen to draw and carve the flower patterns going right through the border. Simply stop the border at a safe distance from both sides of the flower. It isn't absolutely necessary that you do the same, but I believe it adds a little interest and has a nice effect.

Step 4: Transfer the pattern onto the wood. Notice in the pattern that I do not bother including the veins or folds because their placement is arbitrary, which allows you personal choice. Also notice the addition of stab impressions, which are created by using the stab knife.

If this floral pattern is the pattern you have chosen and you have it all drawn out, then let's get chipping away! If you have decided to carve the rosette pattern, let's move on to the drawing.

Finishing up: When the carving is done, you are ready to add a finish. First, remove any pencil marks with an eraser or a light sanding. As with the Napkin Holder project, I have chosen a clear finish of polyurethane. This finish lets the natural beauty of the butternut come through and offers excellent protection. Three light coats from an aerosol spray can followed by a light sanding and then two or three more light coats will do the trick. Satin or matte are my preferred types of polyurethane. If your planter will be in a window, use a brand that specifies protection from ultraviolet light.

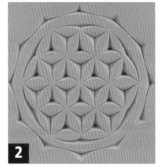

The rosette on the left has been carved in the positive and has been finished with urethane spray. The one on the right has been carved in the negative and has not had a finish applied.

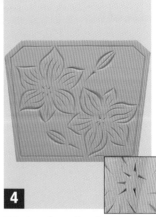

You can choose to carve the flowers through the border. Doing so adds interest and creates a nice effect.

This free-form floral pattern works well on the front, the back, or the sides. I've added stab impressions for interest.

Chip Tip

When deciding whether to carve a pattern in either the positive or the negative, it is often a good idea to carve examples of both on a scrap piece first. The final appearance can be dramatically different, as the Step 2 photos show.

HOW TO DRAW AN INTERLOCKING CIRCLE ROSETTE

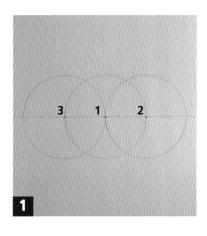

1

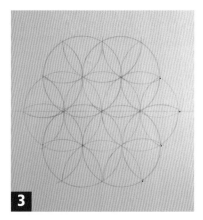

3

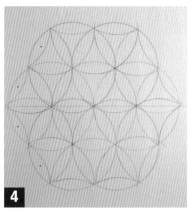

4

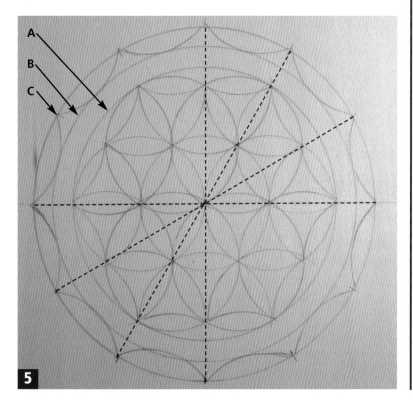

5

Step 1: Draw a horizontal line. Set your compass at a ⅜" radius and draw three circles as shown. All circles should be touching each other. To accomplish this placement, set your compass point at points 1, 2, and 3.

Step 2: Draw four more complete circles by placing your compass point at points 4, 5, 6, and 7. Make sure that you do not move the compass radius setting or your rosette will get out of alignment.

Step 3: You will have noticed that, in the last step, you created petals within the center circle. The next step is to create petals within all of the circles. To do this, keep the same exact compass radius and place the compass point where indicated by the red dots. Continue to walk your compass around the rosette and complete all of the petals as shown. Notice that I have not drawn any lines outside of the circle area.

Step 4: Once your rosette resembles the one shown in the previous step, it is time to add the petals around the outer circumference. I have placed red dots in a few of these so that you will know exactly which ones I am referring to. While it is possible to use your compass to draw these outside petals, I prefer to use that magic template I keep referring to. Isn't it amazing how often that little washer/template comes in handy!

Step 5: The final step in drawing the rosette is to draw in the outer circle. Place your compass back in center of the rosette and open it so that the circle will touch the outer edges of all of the circles. I have labeled this circle A in the illustration.

The next step is to draw the border. Keeping your compass in the center of the rosette, draw a circle 5mm outside the rosette, and then draw another circle 5mm outside that circle. I have indicated these two circles as B and C.

Use a 6" ruler to draw in the points where the petals will meet along the outer border circle. Notice that I have drawn a red dotted line to indicate how to line up the reference points. Any idea what to use to draw in the border petals?

Chip Tip

Don't get too frustrated if your compass work isn't exact. It will take some practice to make it perfect.

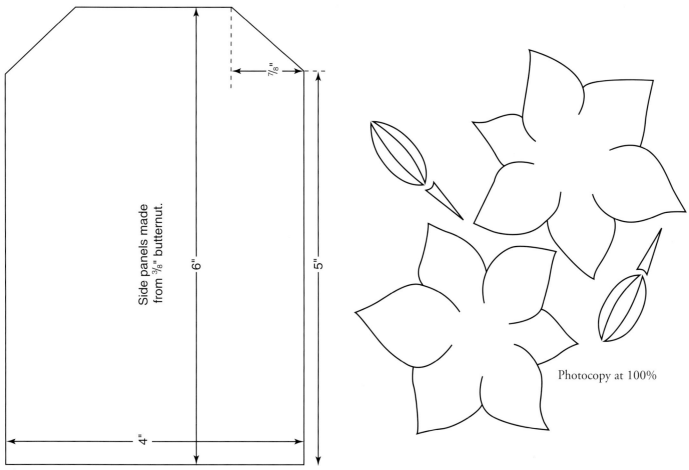

Side panels made from ³/₈" butternut.

⁷/₈"

6"

5"

4"

Photocopy at 120%

Photocopy at 100%

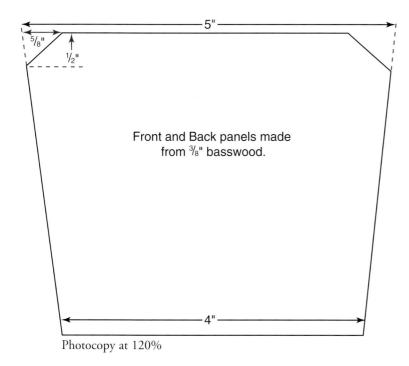

5"

⁵/₈"

¹/₂"

Front and Back panels made from ³/₈" basswood.

4"

Photocopy at 120%

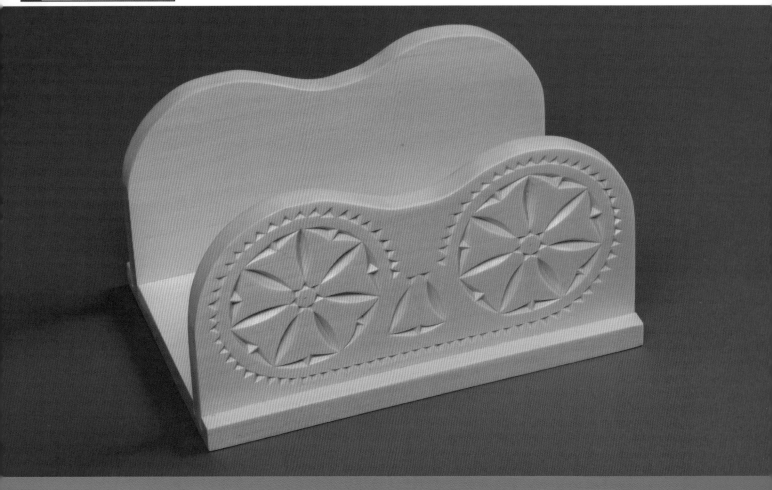

PROJECT 3: LETTER HOLDER

DESIGN INSPIRATION

My work desk is always cluttered. My wife's writing desk at home is always cluttered. My daughter's desk at the bank where she works is always cluttered. Apparently, my entire family lives in clutter. While I am not convinced that this little project will rid us of the problem, it sure will help to keep a few things in order. The shape of this project will start to challenge your design skills. Use the pattern I offer or challenge yourself to create your own. Whichever you choose, your project may help to unclutter your life and let you live happily ever after.

Use this letter holder on your desk in the office or at home. If you are making it for a gift, try including a small sign that reads: "Letters and Cards in Front, Bills at the Back."

The base of this holder has been slotted to hold the front and back panels. You might consider having the front and back panels attached to the outside of the base if you are making your own and have limited woodworking tools. If you make a slotted holder, dry-fit the pieces to ensure a good fit, and then carve them before you do the final assembly. I suggest this because the little overhang at the bottom presents a bit of a carving challenge and the panels do not have any support at the top, which could cause you trouble when you're carving.

MATERIALS

Wood: Basswood

Base: 4" x 6" x ⅜" (if gluing panels without hang-over then make the base only 3¼" wide)

Front and Back Panels: 3" x 6" x ⅜" (if gluing panels without hang-over, make the panels a little wider)

Step 1: First establish and draw the centerlines for both vertical and horizontal dimensions. Then, divide the two vertical sections into two sections as shown.

Step 2: Begin drawing the rosettes using your compass. This rosette divides the circle into seven equal parts. Directions for dividing a circle into seven equal parts are in Chapter Ten: Rosettes. Use a radius of 1" for the initial circle so that you will have enough space to draw the border later.

Set your compass at a 1" radius and place the compass point at the red dot to draw the outside circle.

These next steps are to establish the correct setting for our compass. If you simply kept the same compass radius and started to make full arcs within the circle, you would end up with a six-point rosette. The seven-point rosette leaves an uncarved center area and creates seven bell-shaped designs.

Step 3: Draw a 2" circle by placing the compass point at the established centerline. Without changing the compass setting, place the point at the intersection of the centerline and the circle just drawn as indicated by the red dot. With the compass point at the red dot, make small arcs on the circle perimeter as indicated by the red arrows.

Use a ruler and align the intersections where the two arcs meet the circle perimeter as indicated by the red dotted line. Do not draw the line; simply align the arcs with your ruler. Make a small mark where the ruler crosses the center horizontal line as indicated by the blue arrow.

Now, put your compass point at the intersection indicated by the blue arrow and adjust the compass radius to the distance between that blue arrow intersection and either of the red arrow intersections.

With the radius you have just established on your compass, you are now ready to divide the circle into seven equal parts. Regardless of how careful you were in executing the proceeding steps, it is very likely that your new radius will not be exact. If this happens, don't fret; there is a way to make up for any misalignments.

Step 4: Place the point of the compass at the intersection of the horizontal line and the circle perimeter as indicated by the red dot. Draw the red arc. Move your compass point clockwise to where the arc you just drew meets the circle perimeter as indicated by the blue arrow. Draw the orange arc. Move your compass point to where the arc you just drew meets the circle perimeter as indicated by the green arrow. Draw the next two arcs in the clockwise direction so that you end up with four arcs as pictured.

Step 5: To draw the remaining three arcs, we are going to go back to the first arc we drew. This time we'll work in a counterclockwise direction.

Place your compass point at the intersection indicated by the red dot and draw the red arc. Move your compass point to where the arc you just drew meets the circle perimeter as indicated by the blue arrow.

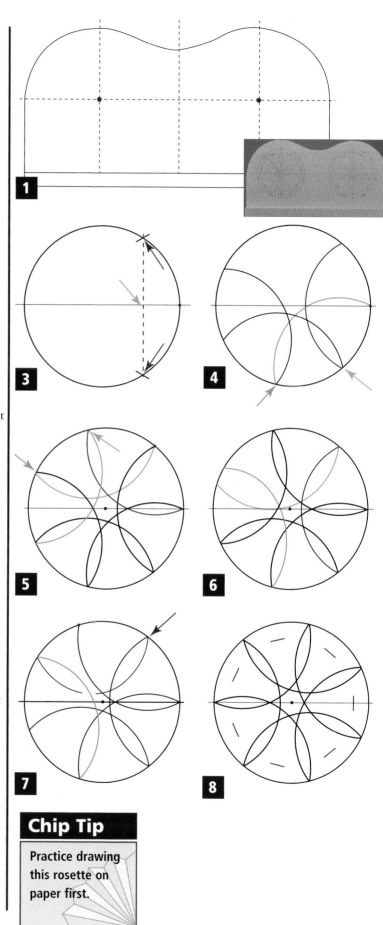

Chip Tip

Practice drawing this rosette on paper first.

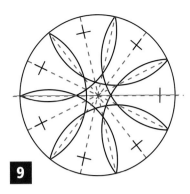

9

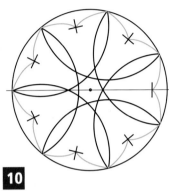

10

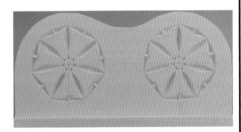

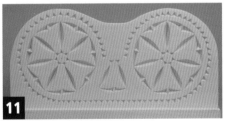

11

The top photo is what your letter holder will look like without a border. Now, look at the bottom photo—see the difference a border makes. Notice that I have also added another bell in the center. This center bell was simply copied with tracing paper from a rosette bell.

Before you draw the blue arc, see if it will meet exactly with the other two arcs drawn previously. If they do not meet exactly, don't draw the blue arc yet—read the instructions in Step 6 first.

If they do meet exactly, draw the blue arc. Move your compass point to the intersection indicated by the green arrow and draw the orange arc to complete the pattern. Your circle is now divided into seven equal parts and should look like the rosette pictured here.

Step 6: I mentioned in Step 5 that before you draw the blue arc, you should see if it will meet exactly with the other two arcs. If you had actually drawn the arc, it might look something like the blue one here. Notice how the blue arc meets the red arc, but it does not meet the green arc. If this is similar to the problem you have, move on to Step 7 for a possible solution.

Step 7: Place your compass at the intersection indicated by the red dot. If the compass meets the intersection indicated by the red arrow perfectly, then draw only half of the arc. You will notice that the arc shown only goes to the center of the circle.

Move your compass point to an area close to the blue dot. Establish the exact location of this blue dot by moving the compass point along the perimeter until the arc will perfectly meet the green arc. Now draw that half of the arc. You will find that the two half arcs meet almost perfectly in the center. Use this same technique to draw the final arc.

Step 8: Draw the bottom of the bells and clappers. To do this, first mark the length of the clappers. Use your compass to draw small arcs approximately 5mm inside the perimeter, shown in red.

Step 9: Mark the center of each bell bottom with a small pencil mark. To find the center, either use a ruler and align it with the petal on the opposite side and the center of the rosette as indicated with the red dotted lines or measure between the two petals.

Step 10: Draw the small blue arcs to form the bottom edges of the bells. Notice that they are arcs and not just straight lines. Draw two arcs per bell from the outside to the mark made in Step 9.

Step 11: At this point, you can either start carving or draw your border. If you were able to draw the seven-point rosette, I have no doubt that you can figure out how to draw the border all by yourself. If you have used all of the measurements given for this project, you will find that a border 4mm wide fits nicely. The little triangular chips in the border complement the triangular chips separating the tops of the bells and tie the entire pattern together.

Finishing up: I have chosen a clear spray finish of polyurethane. If you know where your letter holder will be doing its job, you might consider staining it to match the area. This pattern would also lend itself to reverse finishing.

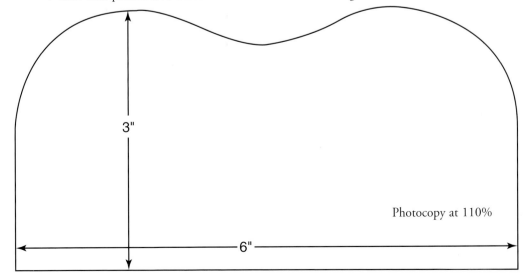

3"

Photocopy at 110%

6"

PROJECT 4: TRINKET BOX

The trinket box is a preassembled and commercially made item. It has hinges and a clasp that will not interfere with the carving. An important feature is that the box has been glued together rather than nailed together, so there is no danger of damage to my knife blade while I'm carving. Get the box ready by thoroughly sanding it with 120-grit, then 220-grit, and finally 320-grit sandpaper.

MATERIALS

Wood: Butternut

Preassembled trinket box: 5½" wide x 11" long x a little more than 3" in height

DESIGN INSPIRATION

When I was first introduced to Peg Couch, the mother of the recipient, she told me that she likes patterns with a foliage theme. Peg is a young woman with two children to look after—one is a husband and the other is a toddler by the name of Sam. Knowing these things, I had lots of information for a project: the theme (foliage), the wood (butternut, because it displays free-style motifs well), the recipient (Sam, because I love children), and the item (a trinket box because all boys and girls need a place to keep their treasures).

1

2

3

4

5

Having the leaves flow into the lid is not difficult to do and offers a nice touch.

Step 1: My first task was to determine the font style for the name "Sam" and where to locate it. Getting opinions from others is a good idea. When I asked Cindy, our general manager at Chipping Away, for her opinion, she suggested using the title "Sam's Things."

Printing out the words in the actual size helps in making the font style decision, and I usually select two or three fonts from my computer to choose from. Sam is a toddler, so I chose a very relaxed, carefree style and decided that one-inch-high lettering across the top would look just about right.

Draw the trinket box top on paper; then draw both the vertical and horizontal center reference lines. Print out the wording and position it on the paper using the reference lines to make sure the size is suitable.

Step 2: Draw a line 1cm in from the edges to represent the outside frame on the top of the box.

Step 3: With the frame established and the two center lines drawn, we have created four equal sections. Let's draw a foliage, or leaf, pattern in just one section and then flip it over both horizontally and vertically to fill in the other sections. Remember, all of these steps so far are only on paper and not on the actual project. Here is a leaf pattern drawn to half scale that will fit one section of the top. Draw this on tracing paper, and then flip it over to make all four sections as shown.

Another reason for drawing the pattern to fit in one-quarter sections is that we can use it on the front, back, and sides of the box as well.

Step 4: This pattern does not require a straight-line chip to frame it because we will create them automatically when we carve the outside portion of the leaves. I indicated the carved-out areas along the outside edges so that you know what I am referring to. All of the red areas will be carved out.

When we carve the leaves, we will also add some veins or folds in each. It really is not necessary to draw the veins because their placement is arbitrary and flexible.

Step 5: We are ready to transfer the pattern onto the box now. First, draw all of the outside frames 1cm in from the outside edges on the top, the front, the back, and both sides. When drawing the patterns on the front, the back, and both sides, you will find that the tops of some of the leaves will be on the lid portion where the box opens. This positioning is fine because we will carve the pattern right through and onto the lid. Don't be afraid to alter the drawing to fit the actual box you are working on. You can make slight changes to the size of the leaves without changing the overall appearance.

Just about all of the carving is done holding the knife in position one. There may be a few times, especially with butternut, when the wood wants to split with the grain and ahead of the knife. If you suspect or even witness this splitting, switch to position two and carve in the opposite direction.

The leaves will be more attractive if you vary the width of the chips as you carve. See how I have made each outline start with a sharp point that widens as it flows along the edge and then goes back to a sharp point. Notice that the veins carved into the center of each leaf curve in the same direction as the leaf appears to curve. This same concept of varying the width is carried over in the lettering and results in the entire pattern coming together nicely.

Finishing up: This butternut box with a foliage design lends itself nicely to a light stain. Match your stain to the box's display shelf. Golden Oak, Pecan, and Mahogany stains will also look attractive.

Photocopy at 110%

Chip Tip

Carve the back of your project. You never know when it might be placed on a dresser or a cabinet with a mirror that reflects the back of the box.

Chip Tip

How is your knife performing? Is it cutting cleanly and without unnecessary effort? Are the sides of the chips clean and smooth? If you are experiencing any difficulty, it could mean your knife needs to be stropped.

If your knife is fine and you are still having trouble with clean cuts, check the wood itself—has it become too dry? Remember that a moisture content of 10% is ideal and makes carving much easier. See Chapter One: Choosing the Wood for more information.

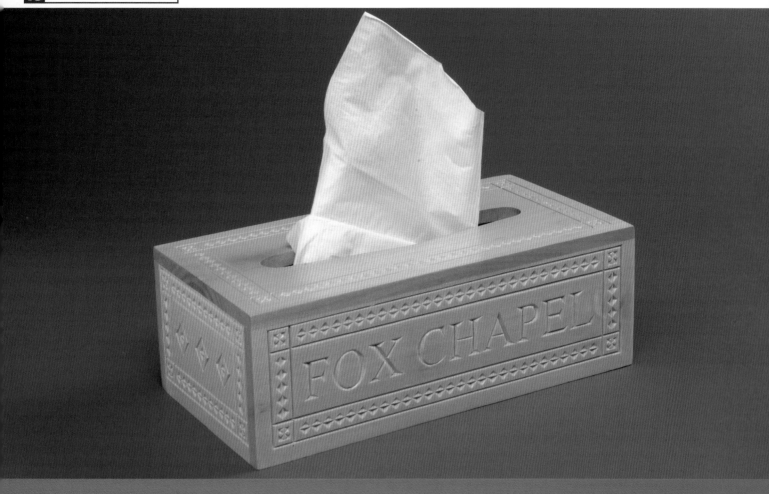

PROJECT 5: TISSUE BOX HOLDER

DESIGN INSPIRATION

This project will get used often whether in the home or office. This particular box is for the publisher of this book, Fox Chapel Publishing, in Pennsylvania. For this project, I plan to use a geometric border and basswood.

So far I have chosen the project (the tissue box), the border (geometric), and the wood (basswood). Now I need a specific geometric border and center design. I can picture the tissue box in the Fox Chapel reception area, the boardroom, Alan Giagnocavo's office (Alan is the boss), or being passed around to whomever seems to be suffering the most from a head cold or allergies.

With this information, I have decided upon a negative diamond pattern because it is attractive and because the sharp center ridges in the diamonds demonstrate carving skill. You can find this pattern in Chapter Six: Standard-Sized Borders, including how to draw it (See page 33). My center design will simply be the lettering "Fox Chapel" in a Roman font. This lettering will do nicely for the front and back. The top will not provide enough room to carve without looking cluttered. On the ends, a variation of the negative diamonds would tie everything in nicely.

Our tissue box holder is an extremely popular item for chip carving. If you wish to make the box yourself, I have offered the measurements in the Materials List as well as the pattern for the slot. You can also purchase the box in kit form and glue it together yourself. Either way, I suggest doing the complete assembly and sanding first, then doing the chip carving. The wood you choose will depend on your pattern. Because I will use a geometric design for this project, I have chosen basswood.

MATERIALS

Wood: Basswood

Top: 5⅝" x 11" x ⅜"

Sides: 3¾" x 11" x ⅜"

Ends: 3¾" x 5¼" x ⅜"

All of these dimensions are finished dimensions. Take into consideration that I am using a kit. The kit, rather than using butt joints, has blind rabbet joints to secure the sides and ends. I have shown a closeup of the joint here.

Step 1: Once the tissue box is assembled and sanded, I can begin the layout of the border. I am going to use a standard 4mm square border with a 2mm straight-line chip on both sides to frame it. Again, this pattern and layout is explained in Chapter Six: Standard-Sized Borders.

Measure in 1cm from all of the edges and, using a good ruler or T-square, establish the first line, indicated by the red arrow.

Step 2: Measure and draw in the other reference lines. The two outside lines are 2mm apart, then there is a 2mm space, then two rows 4mm apart, then another 2mm space, then two inside lines 2mm apart. Draw this layout on the top, sides, and ends. Do not draw the 4mm vertical lines, which will make the center squares, just yet.

Step 3: Now I have to figure out how much room to leave between the innermost layout line and where the 4mm squares will begin. I have indicated that space with a blue arrow. The ideal space would be 2mm because it would keep the same layout format, but it may have to be adjusted depending on the measurement between the two ends.

Measure the distance between these two inner lines. My box measured 227mm. Because I am using the standard 4mm squares and each diamond will be two squares (2 x 4mm = 8mm), I will divide the 227mm by 8mm and arrive at 28.375mm. Therefore, I can make 28 diamonds and end up with (28 x 8mm = 224mm) 3mm left over. Remember, I want to leave a space, indicated by the blue arrow a little earlier. This is almost too good to be true. I will leave a space of 2mm at each end and then draw the 28 diamonds, making one of the diamonds only 7mm wide instead of 8mm wide. If you think this narrow diamond will make much of a difference, I challenge you to find it in the finished carved row.

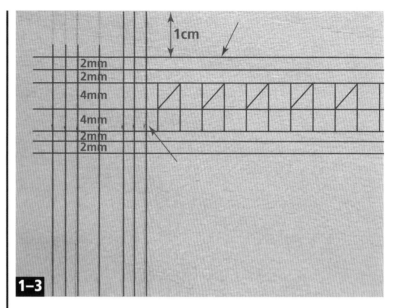

1–3

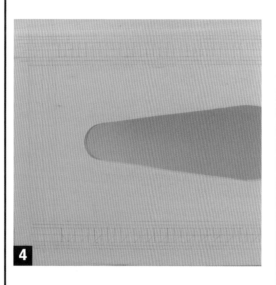

4

Chip Tip

When laying out a border pattern, some carvers prefer to start with a center line and draw the 4mm or 8mm squares outward. This method gives you exact squares, but you will end up with a border that is not exactly the same distance from the outer edge of the project on all sides. The method described here will give exact outer edge measurements.

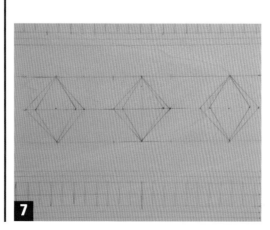

7

Chip Tip

When I carve this project, I will hold the box between my knees and therefore carve the top first and the front and back next, saving the ends for last. Using this sequence will help to prevent the sharp ridges in the center of the negative diamonds from breaking out unnecessarily.

A really good tip: If I have a project with a particularly delicate carved area, I will protect that area by covering it with a stiff piece of cardboard (a cereal box side or the back of a writing pad) and taping the cardboard in place with masking tape.

Step 4: Draw the squares on the ends of the top by performing the same measuring methods and calculations. They work out pretty well.

You can see in the photo, which has the top border drawn out, that there is very little room for additional patterns or carving without the top appearing cluttered.

Step 5: Now it's time to draw the borders on the front and back. Since the length is the same as the top, use the same measurements for the top and bottom border as you used on the top of the box. Then, draw the side borders. Again you will find that the measurements won't give you much of a challenge. I am not sure how we got so lucky on this project; it isn't always this close.

Step 6: It is now time to add the lettering. I highly recommend that you read Chapter Thirteen: Lettering before you carve, or even draw, out your lettering. I have chosen a Roman font, as mentioned earlier, and have decided that 1"-high letters are just about perfect. To make sure I get the lettering absolutely centered, I draw the letters on tracing paper and not on the box. Draw the name exactly as you want it to appear on the box, including the correct spacing between the letters and the correct spacing between the words, or initials, if that's the case. Make sure you have a bottom line so everything is exactly even. Draw a line dividing the length and width in half to use as a reference for positioning. Now draw a center line for both length and width on the box itself that you can use as a reference. Then, trace the pattern onto the box using graphite paper (See Chapter Twelve: Getting the Pattern onto the Wood for how to transfer patterns.).

Step 7: The next step is to draw out the ends of the tissue box. Draw the borders first if you haven't already. Making the overall pattern uniform and tied-in is much more pleasing than just throwing something in to fill space. I avoid mixing geometric shapes with free-form motifs in most cases. If your project is completely free-form, keep the same pattern theme throughout. Let's draw some diamond-shaped patterns on the ends to keep the same theme and present an attractive-looking tissue box that Alan will be happy to display.

Finishing up: I used Varathane Professional Urethane in Satin, applied by an aerosol can, to finish the box. See Chapter Fourteen: Finishing for more details.

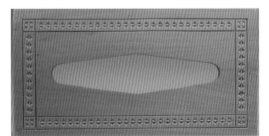

Here is the finished top.

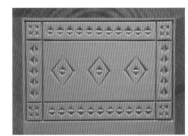

The ends also came out well.

Photocopy at 100%

PROJECT 6: MAILBOX

The design I have chosen for the mailbox itself is actually quite similar to the one now hanging near our front door. This one is made of basswood, but butternut would also be very attractive and practical. If you are a woodworker, or know one, you should be able to make the mailbox without much difficulty. The measurements are offered in the Materials List. If you are not a woodworker and do not have one for a friend, pick up a mailbox in a style to your liking from a source of your choice. I think you will like the pattern I have come up with and will find it easily adaptable to just about any design and size of mailbox you choose.

DESIGN INSPIRATION

Last year, my wife brought home a yellow pine mailbox that she had purchased at the local farmer's market. For some reason, she thought our rusted, 20-year-old, brass-plated box needed to be replaced. When I was carving the new one, I thought that when I wrote another book, it would make a good project. Here we are!

We will not need a mailbox for another 20 years, however. Right now, I have a good idea for a project, but I need a recipient. In fact, I need to know who will be getting this mailbox before I can even think of a pattern or theme for the carving. Ah ha! I remembered a little note at the end of an e-mail that I recently received from Shannon, telling me she was in the process of building a new home. Shannon is married, has two sons, four dogs, three cats, two fish, and probably a couple of birds as well. She needs a new home, and every new home should have a new mailbox. Problem solved. As a matter of fact, deciding that Shannon should get the box also provided the concept for the pattern. How so? Shannon's last name is "Flowers." How easy is that!

MATERIALS

Wood: ½"-thick Basswood

Back: 10" high x 14" wide

Front: 5¾" high x 14" wide

Ends: 6½" high at the back and tapered to 5½" high at the front
x 5¼" wide

Top: 5½" wide x 14½" long, which is then cut into two pieces to allow for a piano hinge. Top should overhang front and ends ¼".

Bottom: scrap piece cut to fit within

1

2

3

As with previous patterns, it really isn't necessary to draw in each and every detail like veins, stab knife impressions, etc.

4

Step 1: The first thing we must decide is what text, if any, we want and, if we do want text, what size and style of lettering we will need. For a mailbox, what could be more appropriate than the family name of the people living there? Because "Flowers" is the name, we will make "flowers" our design theme. The lettering style should therefore be flowing, warm, and friendly. I have included the word "Welcome" in this same style as another option. Also, it should not be too formal, too bold, or too delicate. My choice, once again found in my computer, was printed in various sizes until I found the appropriate one.

Draw the horizontal and vertical centerlines on both the mailbox and the working paper to ensure perfect positioning. Transfer the lettering using graphite paper. The capital *F* is 1¾" high, the *l* is 1⅜" high, and the heights of the remaining letters were determined by my computer.

Step 2: Now decide how far in from the edges of the box you want your straight-line chip frame to be. I chose to come in 1cm; the frame itself will be 2mm in width. Once you've decided, draw it on the box wherever you will be carving, which I suggest will be pretty much the entire surface, except for the back that has the scalloped edge.

Step 3: Trace the flowers, butterflies, and scroll I offer or trace your own patterns onto the wood. I do not draw perfect free-form patterns because I believe that I can carve better than I can draw and therefore can correct any imperfections as I carve out the pattern. If you are uncomfortable with imperfect free-form patterns, go ahead and use any templates, French curves, and drawing tools that you feel are necessary.

Step 4: Notice, on the back panel, that I have flipped the branches and the flowers so that they face each other. The scroll on the back has the illusion of being smaller than the one on the front, but they are both the same size.

Finishing up: The finish on this project is an exterior-quality finish made by Varathane called Diamond Wood Finish and is a Semi-Gloss Luster. It offers good UV protection.

Photocopy at 100%

Welcome

PROJECT 7: CHEESE AND CRACKER TRAY

DESIGN INSPIRATION

Because this project will be used to serve food when the recipient is entertaining guests, the finish must be nontoxic but provide sufficient protection for the wood. I chose a clear finish rather than a stain because a clear finish has the appearance of being bright, shiny, and clean.

We have the project and the finish; now we must decide who the recipient is and what type of motif and border would be appropriate. This one is for Gina Bepko, a woman whom I've had the pleasure to work with.

Now for the pattern. Because the tray will be "handled," we do not want anything too delicate or fragile. Because the actual area to be carved is fairly small (approximaely 6½" x 7¾"), the motif cannot be too bold. It would be nice to identify it as being for Gina, but there isn't room to carve a complete name. Why not carve a B for Bepko? A rosette could be carved in the center with a matching border that could also be used on the sides and handles. The B can go in each of the four corners between the rosette and the borders. Cool!

This project requires good woodworking skills to build, or you can purchase one in kit form that's ready to assemble. If you choose to build it yourself, or to have a woodworker friend have a go at it, then use the dimensions and tips on page 103.

The nature of this project is such that I recommend carving it before assembly. You should dry-fit the pieces to make sure everything will go together nicely and with very little final sanding necessary to have the joints meet perfectly. When doing the dry-fit, you should also have the ceramic tile and the wooden insert in place so that you can mark exactly where your border edges will be located. Mark the side and end edges at the same time.

MATERIALS

Wood: Basswood
Bottom: 8⅛" x 13½" x ¾"
Sides: ⅝" x 13⅛" x ¾"
Ends: 1" x 9⅛" x ¾"
Insert: ⅝" x 8" x ⅜"
Ceramic Tile: 5⅞" x 7⅞"

Step 1: Draw the standard border (described in Chapter Six: Standard-Sized Borders) within the recessed area 6mm in from where the sides, handles, and insert will be. You should have already marked those lines when doing the dry-fit. This border is also the one we used in the tissue box holder project.

With the border drawn, you will have an area approximately 4¾" x 5¾" in the center for the rosette. Draw a faint line across the center of that area. Normally, you would plan your design on paper first; however, if you are using my suggested design, go ahead and draw it right on the wood. Set your compass at a radius of 3cm and draw a 12-point rosette (directions can be found in Chapter Ten).

Step 2: Draw the smallest circle where the smaller petals end; the actual measurement is arbitrary. Each of the other circles is 7mm out from the previous one.

Step 3: Complete the drawing of all the triangular shapes. First, mark the small blue reference dots. Notice how they are found—use a 6" ruler and align it through the center of a small petal on the innermost circle and the center of the corresponding petal on the opposite half of the rosette. Mark the blue dots all around the extreme outside circle and on the third circle in.

Next, mark the small red reference dots on the second circle from the outside. Notice how they are found—use the 6" ruler and align it through the intersection of the triangular chips as indicated.

Step 4: Once you have the reference dots marked in, draw the triangles using the 6" ruler or draw them freehand. The carved rosette should match the one shown here.

Step 5: The Ing border described in Chapter Six: Standard-Sized Borders is very suitable for this design. Both the curved and the small triangle chips tie in nicely with the rosette. For the corners of the border, I chose a negative star, so a variation of the same chip could be used on the insert because the insert is too narrow for a complete Ing design.

Step 6: Putting the B in the corners not only fills the space nicely but also softens the transition from the 90-degree border to the rosette. The font is the same as was used on the mailbox project and goes nicely with the overall design.

I have also continued the Ing border along the edges of the sides. These were quite small to hold while carving, so I held the two of them together with a strip of masking tape down the length.

Finishing up: Satin urethane is my choice. Urethane after a 72-hour curing time is nontoxic. I hope Gina puts it to good use. May I recommend six-year-old cheddar; it's my favorite.

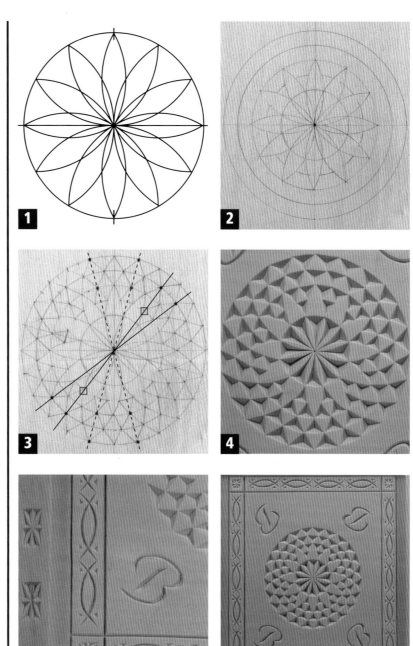

DIMENSIONS FOR TRAY CONSTRUCTION

■ Overall bottom: 8⅛" wide, 13½" long

■ Sides: ⅝" wide, ¾" high, 13⅛" long. Have dado cuts all the way to each end to accept bottom rabbets

■ Ends: 1" wide at top, 9¼" long. Inside cove makes the bottom ½" wide. Have blind dados.

■ Insert (divides ceramic tile from recessed area): ⅝" wide, ⅜" thick, approximately 8" long. Cut to fit snugly once tray is assembled.

■ Ceramic tile: standard 5⅞" x 7⅞" tile from flooring retailer. (If you tell them that you only need one and how you'll use it, they may give it to you for free from their leftover bin.)

GALLERY

Basswood bowl, carving by Wayne Boniface of Kitchener, Ontario

The bowl has a fitted lid that is 9" across and is 4½" tall.

Horse Lover's Box, pattern and carving by Dennis Moor

This is a butternut jewelry box available from Chipping Away in kit form. The rope border and horse pattern are continued on the front and back of the box. There is room between the two horse heads on the front panel to allow for a name to be carved.

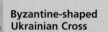

Byzantine-shaped Ukrainian Cross

This unique piece was made in the Ukraine and measures 11" x 5½". Woodcarving is an important and highly developed branch of Ukrainian folk art—highly developed because it has been refined for generations and important because it brings artistic ornamentation beyond ritual and luxury items and moves it into everyday life. Household articles, farm implements, transportation vehicles, as well as religious architecture were made out of wood, and most of these items were embellished with woodcarved designs. The ornamentation was applied to functional and decorative wooden items and consisted of mostly geometric motifs.

Vintage box

This 4" x 6" vintage box is of unknown origin, but notice the angle of the cuts. Two cuts are at 90 degrees with the third, and relief, cut at 45 degrees. This technique is often used by Eastern European chip carvers.

Emilee's Hope Chest,
carving by Dennis Moor

This basswood chest measures 24" x 16" x 16" and has two lift-out trays divided into several sections. The pattern has butterflies on the front and back, hummingbirds on the two sides, and a combination of both on the top. Flowers and foliage are on all sides.

While I was doing some of the carving as part of a demonstration, a lady inquired what I would ask for something like that. I replied "a kiss and a hug," seeing as it was for my granddaughter. She offered payment on the spot!

Butternut rose bowl,
pattern and carving by
Dennis Moor

The bowl is 6" across
and 4" tall.

Welcome plaque in butternut, pattern by Lora S. Irish from *Chip Carving Classics Two* and carving by Dennis Moor

The plaque is just waiting to
have a name or names carved
across the bottom and
be hung on the door. It is
9" x 12" with a plain edge.

Small basswood gift box,
pattern and carving by
Todd Moor

This box only measures
3" x 5" and is great for
presenting small gifts of
jewelry and such. The
flower motif on the sides
is merely mirror-imaged
on the top. Easy and
impressive.

SOURCES OF SUPPLY

The following retailers have a selection of chip carving tools and basswood products:

Chipping Away, Inc.
1-888-682-9801 or 1-519-743-9008
www.chippingaway.com

Woodcraft Shop
1-800-397-2278
www.thewoodcraftshop.com

Highland Hardware
1-800-241-6748 or 1-404-872-4466
www.highlandhardware.com

Woodcraft Supply at their numerous locations
www.woodcraft.com

The following retailers have a selection of basswood products but not carving tools:

Walnut Hollow Farm, Inc.
1-800-950-5101
www.walnuthollow.com

Michaels Craft Stores at numerous locations
www.michaels.com

Hofcraft
1-800-828-0359 or 1-616-847-8822
www.hofcraft.com

The following retailers have a selection of basswood and butternut:

Chipping Away, Inc. (only practice boards for mail order; rough stock for in-store shopping only)
1-888-682-9801 or 1-519-743-9008
www.chippingaway.com

Advantage Trim & Lumber Co.
1-877-232-3915 or 1-716-827-3915
www.advantagelumber.com

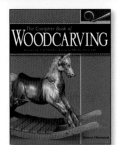